How to Succeed in Your First Job

50 Proven Ways of being Successful in Your First Job and getting Your Career off to a Winning Start

D1615539

O
KELLY
PUBLISHING

Colman Collins

Orla Kelly Publishing
27 Kilbrody,
Mount Oval,
Rochestown,
Cork

To Marie, Ronan and Sarah

About the Author

Colman Collins and his partner Val McNicholas started Collins McNicholas Recruitment & HR Services Group in Galway in 1990. Since then the company has become one of the market leaders in that sector and is now the main recruitment partner for many of the leading multinationals companies based in Ireland. Collins bought out his partner in 2003 and expanded the company significantly before selling it in an MBO transaction in 2015. He has been retained as a Non-Executive Director since the MBO.

Collins is also the Chairman of bizmentors which provides pro bono assistance to over 120 start-up's businesses in the west of Ireland and has been an active mentor to several start-up enterprises.

Prior to setting up Collins McNicholas Collins was a HR professional for 13 years and during that time was HR Director with Nortel Networks in Galway and Westinghouse Switchcontrols in Dunleer, County Louth having commenced his career with Thermo King (Europe) Ltd in Galway.

Collins has a B.Comm degree and post graduate diploma in Social Science from UCD, a diploma in the Psychology of Counselling from NUIG and a post graduate diploma in executive coaching from DIT.

He was a part-time lecturer in HRM in the RTC in Galway (now GMIT) from 1991 to 1995 and was a FCIPD (Fellow of Chartered Institute of Personnel & Development) for the duration of his career.

Contents

Foreword

I have long discussed with business colleagues the persistent lack of preparedness of new graduates for the world of work which they enter through their first job at the start of their careers.

The result too often is a clash of expectations on the part of the fresh-faced graduate employee and the employing company which can lead to disillusionment and disappointment on both sides.

Two different worlds are involved in this engagement:

- The College environment where the student sets out to achieve a Diploma, Degree or Master's qualification in their chosen subject while participating in College life. Even though some may benefit from placements in companies, most graduates have little or no understanding of the corporate world they are about to enter on graduation. Worse than that, they - or their parents - may have unrealistic expectations of the doors open to them simply because they have a third level qualification.

- The Corporate world which involves the collaboration of many individuals to achieve the company objectives through serving customers or clients whether in the commercial, public or not for profit sectors of our society.

The new graduate employee lacks any real preparation for this complex world with resultant frustration all round.

Now, comes a book by Colman Collins which bridges this graduate-employer gap and brilliantly equips the first-time job seeking graduate to navigate with confidence into the corporate world and to progress from there. He draws on his experience as a Human Resources (HR) Director with multinational companies in Ireland and with the Collins McNicholas Recruitment & HR Services Group (which he co-founded) to produce this practical guide for the graduate in their first job.

It is truly a treasure trove of advice for the graduate from preparing for that first interview, to understanding the company culture and values and to a readiness to do certain 'boring' tasks such as filing and record keeping - which, in my own experience, some graduates may consider inappropriate to their educational attainments.

There is an added bonus in Part Two of the book where a range of realities of corporate life such as 'office politics', 'socialising with colleagues' and 'office parties' are analysed and the graduate offered sound advice.

Padraic White
Chairman
Collins McNicholas Recruitment & HR Services
Former Managing Director IDA-Ireland

Introduction

Dear Reader,

If you are embarking on your working life, I hope this book can, in some small way smooth the challenging transition from the world of college to the world of work.

When I started my working life in the mid-70s, there was no such template available to me as I attempted to adjust to the world of work after my time in college. My passage through those early years was very much one of trial and error and I cringe when I think of the many avoidable mistakes I made during that period.

Another reason that prompted me to write this book was that when I was working, I was always interested in why some people had very successful careers while others, who may have had similar or even greater abilities, were much less successful.

In Part 1 of the book, I have outlined 50 ways of being successful at work and my reasons for recommending each of these points. In Part 2 of the book, I have taken 20 typical work-life scenarios, and I have suggested ways you can navigate your way through these particular situations.

Of course, I fully recognise that success at work means different things to different people. I hope this book will encourage you to consider what it means to you. I hope it will also help you recognise that there are sacrifices involved in being successful at work – particularly as you climb the corporate ladder. I suggest you periodically ask yourself whether your definition of success is changing as your personal circumstances change.

In writing this book, I do not lay claim to being an academic or a management guru. However, I do have over forty years' management experience in fast-paced, ambitious companies in the multinational and SME sectors. Because of this, the book is likely to be of most relevance to a professional starting their career in the private sector. However, I also believe it could be helpful to someone starting their working life in the public sector or to a person commencing work in a clerical or administrative capacity in either the private or public sector.

Whatever your reason for reading this book, I sincerely hope that the advice I have offered will help you to be successful at work on your own terms. If you do get one or two useful pointers that help smooth your transition into the world of work, I will consider my efforts in writing this book to have been well rewarded.

Colman Collins
March 2022

Part 1

1
Select the right job in the right company

1. **Ensure that the company and the job will be a good fit for you before applying for your first job.**

   As Ireland enters into the endemic phase of the COVID -19 pandemic and as the economy begins to expand rapidly there are going to be many opportunities for you to consider as you commence your working life.

2. **Take the time and effort to research the job and the company thoroughly.**

   I am confident that you will greatly increase your chances of securing a good job with a suitable employer if you do the necessary research. If possible, get some insight into the company's mission, its culture, and its values.

3. **Check the company's website or check with the chosen recruitment consultancy.**

   Much of the information about a company is available online. You can usually get a job description from the company directly or from a recruitment agency if one has been selected to fill the vacancy. There is no excuse for not doing some elementary research, and failure to do so will quickly becoming evident at the interview, resulting in you being eliminated from the selection process. This is understandable as no employer wants to recruit a person who doesn't take the time to do such basic research. You also need to bear in mind that the people who interview you probably see the company as an excellent employer and superior to their competitors. They are unlikely to be impressed if they sense that you regard the company as just one of many potential employers of equal merit.

4. **Do you know somebody working in the company?**

If so, ask them what kind of place it is to work in. If it sounds like the kind of company that would be suitable for you, it might be worth your while asking them whether they would be willing to recommend you. If they are willing to recommend you, this could put you at an advantage in terms of getting an interview. When I was in HR, I always welcomed such recommendations, especially if the employee making the recommendation was well regarded in the company. I know many other HR practitioners who would take the same view. This makes sense because a well-regarded employee is only going to recommend a person they hold in high esteem.

5. **Do you know somebody who worked for the company previously?**

If that person is someone whose opinion you value, it may be worth asking them for their impressions of the company. If you know them well enough, you may also feel comfortable asking them why they decided to leave the company to move to a new employer. Their reason may be positive in that they received a promotion in accepting their new job, or there may be a less favourable reason. This may highlight a problem in the company which could be specific to only one department, or it may suggest a more fundamental problem within the company.

6. **Find out what people think of the person who will be your immediate boss.**

   You will get a sense of this if you are invited for an interview, but another opinion may give you an insight into the person, which could indicate whether this is the boss for you. This person may not be your boss in the longer term, but it is worth finding out what the person is like as they will probably be the person who will decide if you successfully complete your probationary period with the company. Perhaps you could find out whether they took the time to develop new employees and whether they were popular within the department, particularly with new hires. Having such a boss could be a big advantage to you in your first job, and it may be an influencing factor in deciding to apply for a position with a particular company.

7. **Be ready to ask questions of the interview panel that may provide answers you may be unable to get elsewhere.**

   If you are invited for an interview, you need to be ready to ask questions which will help you make up your mind as to whether this is the company where you want to start your career. For example, you could ask your prospective boss what their expectations would be regarding what you would need to achieve in the first six months.

   Note: This is not a time to ask about salaries and benefits as the employer is unlikely to be impressed if this is the first question you ask. In any event, graduate salaries in big companies are usually in the same salary range, and you can usually get this information from HR or the relevant recruitment agency.

8. Check the CRO (Companies Registration Office) to determine whether the company is profitable and whether it files its annual returns on time.

There is no point in joining a company that is struggling financially or slow to file its annual results.

9. Find out what you can about how the company is perceived in the locality.

Is it integrated into the community by sponsoring local teams, or is it linked with schools and/or colleges in the area? It should be easy to get information regarding the company's CSR policy (Corporate Social Responsibility), which most companies are much more attentive to nowadays. Sometimes this is a core value of an organisation, but it is often a response to employees who want to feel that their employer is progressive in this area and is seen in this regard in the community. This information helps you to build up a picture of the company and their suitability as a potential employer.

Summary:
Thoroughly research the company and the job you are applying for. The more research you do, the more prepared you will be and the more confident you will be if you are called for an interview. This preparation will greatly increase your chances of being successful at the interview. If you do get to the interview stage, you may be given the opportunity to ask some questions about the job towards the end of the interview. You should avail of this opportunity to get a clear understanding of the requirements of the position.

2

Control those first day nerves

1. **Understand and accept that it is perfectly normal to be nervous on your first day at work.**

   This will be understood in the company as it is normal for a new employee to be anxious to make a good first impression. Try to remember that all of the people you meet on your first day also had a first day there themselves and will understand if you appear nervous.

2. **Minimise your anxiety by arriving at your place of work in plenty of time.**

   This means allowing extra time for your journey, especially as it will probably be at rush hour. It may also mean allowing time to find parking and for getting through security, which can take time, especially in large companies. It never ceased to amaze me if a new employee failed to arrive on time for their first day at work, as it always had the effect of getting the employee's new job off to the worst possible start. It also invariably created a poor first impression with their new employer, inevitably raising concerns that this could be the start of a long-term trend.

3. **Expect to be introduced to several people in your first few hours of work.**

   This can be overwhelming, so it is crucial that you take this in your stride and not be concerned if you find it difficult to remember some or all of their names as this is perfectly normal and to be expected. As I have already pointed out, all of these people were newbies at one stage and were probably just as nervous as you, and they will probably have some empathy for you because of this.

4. **Remember that you were recruited because the interview panel decided you were the best person for the job.**

    Your new colleagues will all want you to succeed because if you are successful, that will add to their department's effectiveness and efficiency and to how it is perceived within the company.

5. **Ask questions of the induction team as they will expect you to have many of them at this stage.**

    Again this is all good and entirely normal and nothing to be self-conscious about.

6. **Introduce yourself to others who are starting on the same day as you.**

    It can be helpful to feel you are not the only newbie. Many a long-term friendship has been formed between two people just because they happened to start a job on the same day.

Summary

The first day in any new job involves a mixture of anxiety and excitement. It is important that you prepare yourself mentally to take the day in your stride. Get your day off to a good start by arriving at work in plenty of time and by introducing yourself to anyone else who is starting work that day. You will be assimilating more new information on your first day and in your first week than at any time you are with the company, so try not to allow yourself to be overwhelmed by it all. I had several first days over the years and invariably found them somewhat daunting, although never as bad as I would have been anticipating the night before.

3
Use your induction time well

Most companies, especially multinational companies, have become very professional in inducting and onboarding new employees.

1. **Be attentive during this process as you will have to assimilate a lot of information in a very condensed period of time.**

   This is a time for asking questions to better understand the company, the department you will be working in, and both its internal and external customers. However, be careful not to ask too many questions as this may irritate the company presenter or some of the other new inductees.

2. **Adapt quickly to the induction process of your new employer.**

   Some companies do most or all of the induction in the first week whereas others wait for a week or two while a new employee settles in before starting the induction process. They do this to reduce the risk of a new employee being overwhelmed by being introduced to too much information too soon. It is important that you are flexible enough to adapt to this process, which is usually structured for maximum effect. Also, companies often run induction programmes biweekly or monthly, which can have a bearing on when you start the programme.

3. **Take detailed notes during the induction process as you cannot expect to assimilate all of the information at once.**

Some people do not take notes, which is unwise as this is a once-off crash course prepared for you and the other new employees. It sends out the wrong message to the programme organisers if they see people failing to take adequate notes.

4. **Take time to get to know the presenters and your fellow inductees as they will be your colleagues from now on.**

This is a great chance to get to know these people who will be colleagues for as long as you and they are employed by the company. As I will cover at a later stage, it is a mistake to limit your contacts to those within your own department, and induction is a readymade opportunity to begin to build a cross-functional network within the company.

5. **Participate fully in the induction programme as most programmes are designed to be very interactive.**

This will add to the programme's effectiveness for everyone – including yourself, your fellow attendees, future attendees, and the programme presenters.

6. **Familiarise yourself with the company goals and how each department contributes to achieving these goals.**

This is an integral part of any induction programme. On the one hand, it gives you the big picture while also indicating where your department and your role fit into that picture. Some people make the mistake of not concerning themselves with issues outside of their role or department. This is a big mistake as individuals and departments are becoming increasingly interdependent and interconnected in all organisations.

7. **Review your notes each evening to identify any areas you feel you need to understand better.**

   This may be the last thing you will feel like doing after a very intensive day, but it is worth the effort as you will be better prepared for the next day of the induction programme.

8. **Complete any evaluation sheets about the effectiveness of the induction programme.**

   This can help the programme organisers as they continually endeavour to improve the programme for future attendees. In my experience, constructive criticism and helpful suggestions are nearly always welcome. Any constructive comments you make to the programme organisers will reflect well on you and should add to the positive first impressions you have created at the induction stage.

Summary:

The induction process is an effective way for companies to impart a lot of information in a very short period of time. As such, it is vitally important that you are very attentive and use your time on the programme to fast-track your introduction into the company. In my experience, employees who stand out in the induction programme often become some of the top performers in the company.

4
Adopt company culture and company values

A. Company Culture

Every company has its own distinct culture, and if you are to succeed in that company, you need to buy into that culture. This is based on the assumption that you took the time to check out the company culture before you applied for the job, and it is a culture that appeals to you.

1. **Recognise that company culture is more powerful and influential on a day-to-day basis than mission statements, company vision, and company values.**

   That being the case, it is very important that you are fully in alignment with this culture, or you will not be happy working in this environment and will likely leave the company or be asked to leave it at an early stage in your employment. There is a well-known saying in recent years that, 'Culture eats strategy for breakfast.' This statement accurately reflects the importance of culture in any organisation.

2. **Accept that it is nearly impossible for an employee to bring about change to company culture, particularly in a large company.**

   Trying to change company culture is futile. The exception might be in a small indigenous company where you are part of the senior management team and you have been with the company for several years. Remember, all established companies which have developed their own unique culture over many years are often very successful and, as a consequence, see no reason to change that culture.

3. **Culture can best be described as 'the way we do things around here.'**

   This can vary hugely from one organisation to another, which is why I highlight it as an important area of research before you apply for a job with any company. Some companies are very hierarchical in their organisational structure, whereas others are very flat – whichever it is, it reflects and influences the culture of those organisations.

Summary:

Be sure you are in alignment with the company culture before you join the company. If you join a company without researching its culture and it is one you cannot align with, then I suggest you look for another position elsewhere because even though company cultures do change over time, such changes are often slow and incremental.

B. Company Values

Company values are also very important and usually reflect the culture, mission, and vision of the company.

1. **It is very important that you demonstrate these values in your dealings with external and internal customers.**

   In a well-managed company, values are more than aspirational statements. Every manager and employee is expected to continually reflect the company values in their internal and external interactions.

2. **Values are usually easily understood, and you should be able to adopt them as part of your modus operandi.**

   Typically, companies have five or six values which are usually expressed in simple language. These would generally be seen as good business practice. It is not unreasonable for your employer to expect you to reflect these values in how you do your job every day.

3. **Demonstrate company values, even if these are not always practiced by company management.**

   Unfortunately, it is true that companies often fail to live up to their value statements, especially when times are tough. Notwithstanding this, as a professional, you should still try to demonstrate these values in all of your interactions, both internal and external. The COVID-19 pandemic and the economic crash in 2008 clearly illustrated which companies and organisations lived up to their values in times of crisis. Unfortunately, these difficult times also highlighted which ones did not act in accordance with their values. Worse still, it resulted in some organisations behaving in ways that were diametrically opposed to their much-touted values. An organisation which blatantly fails to live up to its values will have a major task on its hands to rebuild trust with its employees and with its clients. The Irish banking sector is a case in point where more than fourteen years after the banking crisis of 2008, all banks are still struggling to build any significant level of trust with their customers.

4. **Adherence to company values is usually taken into consideration in the performance management process.**

   This is usually the case in well-managed organisations, and it is another good reason why you should demonstrate company values at all times.

Summary:

Company values are important. As a new employee, you should demonstrate these values in all of your internal and external interactions. They are sometimes not as evident as company culture, especially in indigenous companies. If a company takes time to review its values, you should contribute to that process if you are encouraged to do so.

5

Communicate clearly and effectively

A. Oral Communications

1. **Think before you speak.**

   People do not have time to listen to ideas that have not been thought through before they are articulated. Keep your sentences short. Use action verbs. Keep things simple, jargon-free and ensure your message is clear.

2. **Learn the skill of speaking clearly and succinctly.**

   Time is precious, and attention spans are becoming increasingly short. You must learn to get your message across quickly and in very simple terms.

3. **Be aware of the importance of speaking with conviction.**

   Even if your idea is good, it may not be accepted if you fail to present it in a convincing manner. Many good ideas have been lost because they were presented in a tentative or in an unconvincing manner. If you do not speak with conviction, how do you expect others to be convinced by what you say? Speaking with conviction means speaking slowly, clearly, deliberately, confidently, and pausing to highlight your main points.

4. **Remember your body language is very important when you speak.**

   I will cover this in greater detail when I address the subject of making presentations, but for now, I would like you to take on board a few brief points. You should always make and maintain eye contact. You should maintain an alert posture and avoid inadvertent body movement, such as shuffling or slouching, whether sitting or standing. Any such movement is a potential distraction and can take away from the effectiveness of your communication. Use your hands to make your point where relevant.

Summary:

This is an area where you will have already displayed some level of competence in your time in college. However, you must quickly learn to adapt your communication style to the requirements of the business world. You must be clear, concise, and succinct in everything you say, and your tone of voice and body language must be congruent with your message.

B. Written Communications

1. **Keep your emails brief and to the point. If you have to write a detailed report, provide a concise executive summary.**

   Many of the same points which apply to oral communications are also relevant for written communications. Use action verbs and keep your sentences short. Make your call-to-action clear.

2. **Stay clear of jargon as much as possible.**

   Try to avoid using words that are not in daily usage. You may think using unusual words will impress others, but it will be more likely to irritate them and take away from the message you are trying to get across.

3. **Ensure there are no spelling errors.**

   If you use spellcheck, be sure the spelling selected is appropriate to the context. As a former HR Manager, I used to be amazed when I would get applications from professional Quality Managers and Quality Engineers with several spelling errors in their CVs!! Proofread everything before you send it.

4. **Save a draft of an email you are proposing to send when expressing strong feelings concerning an incident that has arisen.**

   You can always send it later, or you may decide to rephrase it to take some of the emotion out of it before you send it. Many a promising career has been stalled or permanently damaged by dashing off an emotive email in the heat of the moment.

Summary:

As with verbal communication, proficiency in written communication is one of the essential skills you will require to be an effective employee. You will have some competence in this area before you start work, but you must adapt your communication style to suit the requirements of the business environment. Ensure your written communications are clear, concise, and accurate. Proofread all written communications before you send them.

6
Demonstrate a strong work ethic

1. **Adopt a strong work ethic from your first day at work.**

   If you do this, it will not only help you in your first job, but it will establish a firm foundation for your working life.

2. **Demonstrate great determination and commitment to initiate and maintain a strong work ethic.**

   It is a sad fact that many people who start out with good intentions are lured into or gradually slip into bad work practices. If this happens in a well-run company, you will either be dismissed if you fail to take significant corrective action or you will fail to make any progress within that organisation.

3. **Be single-minded and results-oriented to withstand attempts by others to get you to slow down and take it easy.**

   This can take on a sinister dimension in some workplaces, where there can be intimidation of people who work hard to prevent them from showing some of their fellow employees in a bad light. The presence of intimidation in any workplace is nearly always an indicator of weak management, and it also suggests an organisation culture that is seriously lacking in accountability. Advise such people that you will report them if they persist in this kind of behaviour.

   Trade unions, particularly in the public sector, are often blamed for condoning or encouraging this kind of behaviour, which undoubtedly happens occasionally. However, for such a culture of intimidation to become established in the first instance, I would argue it indicates a serious failure of management in allowing such practices to take hold in an organisation.

It is nothing short of a scandal to see enthusiastic and highly motivated new employees slowly lose their energy and idealism as a result of threats and intimidation where management turns a blind eye to this totally unacceptable behaviour.

4. **Ensure your hard work is not just a short-term strategy for when you are on probation.**

    Some employees reduce their efforts on completing their probationary period. I would advise against this and strongly suggest taking the long-term view that a robust work ethic should underpin your entire career.

5. **Develop a feeling of justifiable pride in your achievements at work by having a strong work ethic.**

    Many people derive much of their self-esteem from their work. Having a strong work ethic will enhance your self-esteem and this, in turn, will positively influence other aspects of your life. Equally, I would suggest that not having a strong work ethic could permeate and adversely affect other parts of your life.

6. **Do not become a workaholic.**

    In advocating a strong work ethic, I am not suggesting that you should become a workaholic. This would be a very unhealthy development and could lead to failure to develop as a well-balanced human being with a full and rewarding life outside of work. In the past, too many people, particularly men, derived most of their self-esteem from their work and this often had adverse consequences for them and for their families.

7. **Beware of a culture in some companies with an expectation of employees working very long hours most days and working weekends.**

These companies may also cultivate a culture of being continually online so that even when you are at home or on holidays, you are never off-duty. This could lead to a very destructive and unsustainable arrangement, and could result in employees experiencing extreme anxiety and other mental health problems. It should be pointed out that in many companies, this pressure is subtle rather than overt. Should you find yourself in such a work culture, you may be better off looking for another job because as previously outlined, you are unlikely to be able to change such a work culture.

8. **Recognise that the expectations of long hours can be disguised or camouflaged by other attractive features in some companies.**

These attractive features may be evident in a liberal attitude relating to matters such as choice of work attire, provision of a games room or a gymnasium, a well-funded sports and social club, and many other attractive perks. These are very appealing, especially to a young workforce who highly value these kinds of employee benefits. However, it is difficult not to conclude that the real purpose of these benefits is to keep employees at work for as long as possible. Such companies can appear trendy or even funky but working excessive hours is neither desirable nor sustainable as a long-term arrangement.

Summary:

I strongly recommend that you resolve to develop a strong work ethic from day one. Do not give in to any gentle hints or outright pressure, or even intimidation to slow down. Neither should you allow yourself to be sucked into a work culture where you have a very limited personal life. Work hard but let yourself have the time for a full family and social life. In this way, you should succeed in striking a balance that should sustain you for your entire working life.

7
Work with energy and enthusiasm

1. **Display energy and enthusiasm at work from day one.**

   This is a prerequisite for success in your first job, as well as for a successful career. If you do not feel energy and enthusiasm for your work on a regular basis, you need to seriously consider if you are in the right job. You will be working for many years, so it is very important to select a job and a career that you are enthusiastic and passionate about, if possible.

2. **Show you are self-motivated by displaying energy and enthusiasm.**

   Demonstrate you are self-motivated, energetic, and enthusiastic from the start of each working day. If you start the day in this manner, you will find it easier to continue in that vein rather than trying to generate enthusiasm after a sluggish start to your day.

3. **Remember that all managers want employees with these qualities.**

   It makes the job of a manager so much easier if an employee has these qualities. This helps the manager's department be seen in a positive light as departments with a high proportion of energetic and enthusiastic staff are invariably successful.

4. **Demonstrate these qualities to stand out as a person with potential for future advancement within the company.**

   To advance in most companies, you will need energy and enthusiasm. The further up the organisation you progress, the greater the demand is for people who manifest these attributes.

5. **Do not expect to feel energy and enthusiasm every day.**

   Providing you feel energy and enthusiasm most days, these qualities will always define you. As with occasional episodes of low motivation, which is addressed in the next section, it is important that you work through the days of lower than usual levels of energy and enthusiasm. Most people understand that energy levels fluctuate, but once you are generally energetic and enthusiastic, that will be acceptable in most organisations.

6. **Generate some energy and enthusiasm even for the most basic of tasks.**

   There are certain tasks in every job, such as filing or re-cord-keeping, that many otherwise high-performing employees may consider boring. The fact that they may be boring doesn't mean they are not important. Therefore, it is essential to perform such duties diligently even if you are not enthusiastic about them. Many a good career has been adversely affected by poor record-keeping. Many good companies have lost business or even been closed because of a casual attitude to routine but important tasks.

7. **Try to help your boss or a colleague if you are on top of your work and have some free time.**

   This will usually be greatly appreciated. Even if your offer of help is not always taken up, it may be reciprocated sometime when you are very busy and need 'a dig out.' Of course, this must not become a regular occurrence where you may be covering up the poor performance of a boss or colleague. You should be able to quickly recognise if that is the case and take corrective action.

8. **Avoid low-energy people who lack enthusiasm.**

   These kinds of people will hold you back at the very least and, at worst, drag you down. Be polite but limit the dealings you have with such people to the bare minimum.

Summary:

I would encourage you to display energy and enthusiasm from your first day at work. These are two of the most sought-after qualities that employers look for when recruiting or promoting personnel. They are positively differentiating qualities, and you should try to demonstrate them at every opportunity as they will stand to you, not only in your first job but throughout your working life. Be careful that you avoid making the familiar mistake of failing to bring the necessary energy levels to routine but important tasks and limit your contact with low-energy people.

8

Be self-motivated

1. **Look to yourself for the necessary motivation to be successful at work.**

   It is generally accepted nowadays that the responsibility for being motivated, just as it is for being happy, lies with yourself rather than with someone else. Many people look to their manager for motivation, and ideally, all managers should have strong motivational qualities. However, while it is an advantage to have a manager with strong motivational skills, some people make the mistake of blaming their poor work performance on their manager's weak motivational skills. I think this is missing the central point, i.e. it is your responsibility to generate your own motivation. When I started work in the 70s, the thinking was that managers were responsible for motivation, and academic literature often reflected this mistaken view. Having a manager with strong motivation skills is a bonus, but ultimately, you are responsible for your own motivation.

2. **Do not allow yourself to become discouraged if your manager is a weak motivator.**

   I fully appreciate this is difficult, and it may feel like an uphill struggle at times. However, regardless of the weakness of your manager as a motivator, it is still your responsibility to do your best every day. In a situation like this, I would suggest you just get on with your work and trust that the company will identify your manager as a weak link and either develop them or replace them before the problem gets out of hand.

3. Value a manager with strong motivational skills.

If you are fortunate enough to work for such a manager, as well as doing your job, take some time to identify how they motivate their team so effectively. In this way, you may learn skills and develop qualities that could benefit you, should you be promoted into a management position in the future. Such managers often generate great loyalty in their team, which tends to be enduring and can last long after you have stopped reporting to this manager. I recently attended the funeral of a manager I worked for more than forty years ago. I still remember him with great fondness, affection, and appreciation for the interest he showed in me at a formative stage of my career.

4. Accept that there will be days when you may not feel as motivated as usual, and you may even feel demotivated.

I fully understand this and recognise that we are not machines, and we all have a life outside work. If you are worried about something in your personal life, you do not just flick a switch and forget this when you go to work. On days like this, it is important that you do not berate yourself; show yourself some compassion and do your best to contribute as much as you can.

5. Take corrective action if your low motivation persists.

If your low level of motivation persists, it is important that you are proactive about this as it may begin to affect your mental health, as well as your work performance. There may be an Employee Assistance Programme in the company to help employees with personal problems. You may prefer to talk to your own doctor, who may prescribe medication and/or therapy to help you at a difficult time in your life.

Thankfully, there is greater awareness and understanding of mental health issues nowadays, and there is a growing recognition that having a problem is part of our shared humanity rather than an indication that a person just doesn't cut it anymore.

6. **Act as if you are self-motivated or, in more modern parlance, 'fake it til you make it.'**

   Such techniques can work on days when nothing is seriously wrong, but you just don't feel yourself. Try to generate some enthusiasm and apply yourself to your work, and the momentum of this can help you overcome your initial feelings of inertia and get your day started.

Summary:

Decide from day one that you will take responsibility for motivating yourself. Do not let yourself be demotivated by a weak manager. Consider it a bonus if you work for a manager with strong motivational skills. Try to learn and adopt some of their motivational techniques. Be compassionate towards yourself if you are having a bad day but get help if the problem persists.

9

Behave with honesty and integrity

1. **Resolve to act with honesty and integrity from day one in your first job and in your working life.**

   These are among the most important and sought-after qualities that employers look for when recruiting new employees. This is one of the key points I would encourage you to adopt. As such, they are qualities you need to demonstrate from the beginning as a new employee. Your employer thought they saw these qualities in you when they decided to recruit you, so you must try to confirm that impression at every opportunity. Telling lies is one of those offences that can lead to instant dismissal, which nobody wants on their employment record.

2. **Avoid the world of partial truths.**

   In my experience, very few employees deliberately go out of their way to tell a barefaced lie. The situation is usually less clear-cut than that, as employees can easily enter into the grey area of partial truths. This is a dangerous space to get into because if you get a name for being a person who does not tell the whole truth, you probably won't be retained by your employer.

3. **Admit immediately if you make a mistake and seek to rectify your error if you are able to do so.**

   There may well be adverse consequences when you admit to a mistake, but they are likely to be much less severe than if you knowingly seek to cover it up.

4. **Admit if you forgot to do something you were told to do and seek to rectify the oversight as quickly as you can.**

   As a graduate, you will probably escape with a warning if this was a genuine omission, but you are unlikely to be forgiven if you do not admit to the oversight immediately.

5. **Challenge a colleague who attempts to cover up a mistake or who tries to put the blame elsewhere.**

   Advise them that you are aware of the issue and will inform their boss if they do not admit to it immediately. It is a serious mistake to turn a blind eye to something like this because if it subsequently becomes known that you knew about the problem but decided to do nothing about it, you will probably be considered every bit as culpable as your colleague. It will be perceived that you knowingly allowed a problem to continue when you could have reported it and provided management with the opportunity to address it as expeditiously as possible.

6. **Admit to your part of the problem if responsibility for a problem is shared but don't 'take the rap' for someone else.**

   If you know who is responsible for the rest of the problem, then I would advise approaching them and suggesting that you both admit your shared culpability. If the other person won't agree to that, then I suggest you tell them you will be advising your boss of the shared responsibility for this error. A former colleague of mine used to refer to this as 'stabbing someone from the front'!

7. **Do not agree to turn a blind eye to something wrong done by a colleague or friend.**

   Advise them that they need to own up to the issue, or you will bring it to your boss's attention. This may cost you a friendship but that is preferable to you being subsequently seen to have failed to act in the company's best interest as well as in your own best long-term interest. In any event, do you want to remain friends with someone who would behave in this manner and potentially compromise your position in so doing?

8. **Caution a colleague who tries to amend or get rid of some incriminating documentation.**

   It is much better that you do this before they act dishonestly and that you advise them if they follow through on their proposed action that you will report it. As per Section 17, if you are not seen to be part of the solution by doing what I have suggested, you will probably be seen as part of the problem, and you may well lose your job as a result.

9. **Behave honestly if your boss asks you to do something wrong to prevent them being seen in a bad light.**

   This is a very difficult situation and a highly inappropriate position for a person in authority to try to put you in. You must refuse to do what you have been instructed to do, and you must ask your boss to do the right thing. I do realise this is a difficult position to be put in as a new employee, especially where you like your boss and get on well with them, but you must do the right thing and advise them to do the same. It may have adverse short-term consequences for you, but you will emerge from the episode knowing you did the right thing. However, you may also feel the need to move to a new employer if, as is likely, that the relationship with your boss has been irretrievably damaged.

Summary:

In court, when a person is required to give evidence, they are asked to tell the truth, the whole truth, and nothing but the truth. I believe this should be your position regarding being honest at work. It will stand to you in the long run, and this is clearly a situation where you need to take a long-term view. You owe it to yourself and to your present and future employers that you will always be seen as an honest person and a person of the highest integrity. This approach may put you in some difficult positions throughout your working life, but it is most definitely the best approach in the long term.

10
Implement a policy of strict confidentiality

1. **Be strictly confidential in relation to your company, its clients, suppliers, and employees.**

    This applies not just to your first employer, but to any company or organisation that you may subsequently work for.

2. **Most companies have employee handbooks which will contain a policy on the issue of confidentiality.**

    If your company has an employee handbook, then familiarise yourself with this policy. If you are ever in doubt about the confidentiality of any piece of information, take a conservative view and treat that information as confidential.

3. **Be aware that a breach of confidentiality usually results in instant dismissal.**

    The fact that the penalty for breaches of confidentiality is so serious should highlight to any new employee the importance of this issue.

4. **Be aware of specific confidentiality requirements in the following functions: research, production, and HR.**

    Research: You will be exposed to confidential information about the company's current and future products and processes on a daily basis. Because of this and the confidentiality clause in the company handbook, many companies require employees who have access to such sensitive information to sign a non-disclosure agreement (NDA). If you are in this category of employee, you must treat that information as confidential even after leaving that company. This is particularly so if the company you join is a competitor of your former employer.

Finance: The same requirements for confidentiality apply for very obvious reasons. If competitors were to acquire sensitive information about costs or profit margins, it could be very serious for your employer so extreme care is called for in what you say and to whom.

HR: As I know from my time in HR, the requirement for confidentiality is particularly onerous. I believe no professional HR practitioner would deliberately reveal confidential information about an employee or about a former employee. However, the risk is usually not in an HR professional deliberately disclosing sensitive information but rather, in them inadvertently saying something casually to a friend or a family member without considering the potential impact of the information imparted. This issue is particularly sensitive if you live in a small town or village where everyone knows everyone else and where 'news travels fast.' If the imparted information is subsequently shared and the leak is traced back to you, the chances are that you will be dismissed on the spot, and rightly so, even if it was an unintended indiscretion on your part. As the saying goes, 'a shut mouth catches no flies!'

5. **Adopt your professional body's code of practice in relation to confidentiality.**

As a young professional, you should become a member of the most relevant professional body for you and familiarise yourself with, and strictly adhere to, its code of practice relating to confidentiality.

6. **Do not assume there is less need for confidentiality in a company where much general information is available.**

   This is a dangerous thing to assume. You must be very vigilant to ensure that you do not disclose a confidential piece of information that could potentially have a very different impact than the general information that is widely known and freely available. This is very important in any location, particularly in a relatively small town where much is known about the company and where many residents may work in the company.

7. **Be vigilant in social settings when your work or your company come up in conversation.**

   I would urge any employee, especially any new employee to be extremely vigilant and to avoid talking about the company except in the most general terms when you are outside work, particularly if there is alcohol involved.

Summary:

Be confidential at all times. Remember that a breach of confidentiality will often lead to instant dismissal. This will leave a permanent stain on your employment record, which will follow you wherever you go. If you are in any doubt about the confidentiality of any piece of information, take a conservative approach and treat it as being confidential.

11

Become a good time manager

1. **Practice implementing the principles of time management from day one.**

   This will assist you in your first job and will stand to you throughout your working life. We all start the day with the same number of hours available to us at work, but some people differentiate themselves by using this precious resource very effectively. On the other hand, some people may actually work quite diligently but waste their precious time because they spend too much time doing unimportant tasks while ignoring or spending insufficient time on the most important aspects of their job.

2. **Learn and adopt the 80/20 rule.**

   Implementing this rule means that 80% of your time will be spent doing the most important 20% of your work. This means you must be clear and agree with your manager on what your most important objectives are (see Section 24). Ensure that you spend most of your time achieving these objectives. This is common sense, but only the really effective employees operate according to this rule.

3. **Don't start working on the tasks you like unless they are the most important things you should be working on.**

   This is a classic time management issue and is readily understandable as people naturally gravitate towards doing the tasks they like first. You need to overcome this tendency and instead focus on the most important parts of your role.

4. **Don't do the easiest and quickest jobs on your 'to do' list first.**

   If you complete eight out of ten items on your 'to do' list, you are 80% efficient but remember you will be 100% ineffective if you fail to do the 20% of important but more difficult jobs on that list.

5. **Identify the time of day you are most effective and try to do your most important work at that time.**

   Do routine tasks like responding to general emails, filing, or filling in your expenses form when you are not at your most effective. For example, immediately after lunch is such a time for many people.

6. **Learn how to manage interruptions, or your day could easily be hijacked by others.**

   This may mean saying to someone that you are busy at that particular moment and that you will come back to them later at a set time, or it may mean letting the phone ring through to voicemail if you are working on something very important. For people to accept this kind of work practice, it is essential that you come back to them when you say you will.

   Obviously, if your boss comes to you or calls you, you will speak to them, but if they ask you to do something that appears to be less important than what you are working on, you may need to ask them whether they are happy for you to set aside that work in order to do what they are requesting.

   Some interruptions may just be caused by people calling in for a brief (or not so brief!!) chat. It's nice to be friendly to people, but you must not allow your time to be hijacked by others. Non-work-related chats need to be kept to a minimum. The pandemic which resulted in so many people working from home showed us all just how much time in the office is lost through interruptions. These lessons should not be forgotten when you do go back to the office, even if this is on a part-time basis.

7. **Learn to say 'no.'**

This is a key skill of time management but not an easy one to adopt because as a new employee, your natural orientation is to be obliging and do whatever you are asked. However, you must remember to keep your focus on the main objectives of your position as much as possible. If you keep obliging people by taking on new tasks, it is highly likely that your objectives will not be achieved, and you may well be released at or before the end of your probationary period.

8. **Try to only handle each piece of correspondence once.**

A system I found which worked well for me with correspondence was to either do it, ditch it or delegate it. Again such advice comes with health warnings, but the general point is to avoid the habit of shuffling the same paper or re-reading the same emails without making decisions on them. A large 'pending file' is not recommended.

9. **Use the internet or social media at work only for work-related duties.**

Most employers have had to develop strict policies about social media and the internet in general because they have become a serious time waster in many companies and have led to significant losses in productivity in organisations without adequate controls in this area. You are paid to do a job, and connecting with your friends or commenting on social media is time-wasting and most definitely not part of your job.

10. Be brief and to the point in your verbal and written communications.

Most people in well-run businesses are very busy, and because of this, they have a limited attention span. Therefore, you need to be direct, succinct, and to the point in your verbal and written communications. You should also encourage a similar style from people who need to communicate with you.

Summary:

Learn to use your time well from day one. Stick to the 80/20 rule. Learn to manage interruptions. Learn how and when to say 'No.' Be brief and to the point in all of your communications. Learn from people who are recognised as being very effective in their work but who do not appear to be under pressure. Invariably, you will discover that these people are effective time managers.

12

Learn to listen attentively

1. **Do this from day one, as it will be an essential attribute for all of your professional life.**

   Flushed with success after attaining their degree, many new graduates approach their first job with the expectation that they can make an immediate impact in their new job, whereas their employer will want to see how successfully they can make the transition from college life to the world of work. You need to appreciate that all you have at this stage is a strong foundation of education on which to build a successful career.

2. **Recognise early on that you must be willing to look and listen much more than you may have expected to.**

   This can be quite a shock to new graduates, especially as they may not have previously acquired the skill of being a good listener. The sooner you learn this lesson, the quicker you will successfully transition from college life to work life.

3. **Listen attentively during your induction programme.**

   This is your first chance to practice your listening skills, but it is one that some employees do not fully avail of. Some new employees make the mistake of wanting to get the induction period completed as quickly as possible to start making an impact. This is a mistake because this induction period is a way of fast-tracking your introduction into the company and preparing you for the extended period of listening on the job that will immediately follow your induction.

4. Listen, really listen.

I would put this particular quality in my top three pieces of advice for any new graduate. This is hard work as it requires you to give your undivided attention to whoever is speaking to you. You may have thought your listening role was largely over when you finished college but as a young professional, you will hopefully soon realise that there will be much listening involved, especially in the early phase of your new role.

5. Concentrate.

Because everything you learn in the initial few weeks is new to you, it requires your full concentration. The world of work is new to you, so you need to give it your full attention even if you feel overwhelmed at times.

6. Accept if you experience frustration.

It may be frustrating for you as you begin to realise just how little you know and just how much you have to learn. You need to accept this and realise that all of your colleagues had to go through this process when they first transitioned to the world of work.

7. Understand why certain processes were put in place in the first instance before trying to change them.

This means asking questions before rushing off to recommend some changes which may or may not be an improvement.

8. Be patient.

Be like a sponge – absorb everything as you slowly build up an understanding of your role, your department, other departments, and the company as a whole. As the saying goes, you were given two ears and one mouth for a reason!!

You will be anxious to contribute, but you need to accept and recognise how much you have to absorb before you are ready to make an impact.

9. Look on your first three months at work as a period of intense learning.

This is when you start to build up a work foundation on top of the foundation of your college education. By looking at things in this way, you will have the right attitude to prepare you for gradually beginning to make an impact at work.

Summary:

You are a new graduate. You are working with colleagues who have a proven track record acquired over several years. You need to listen closely to them. Graduates who fail to listen end up making several mistakes they could have avoided had they taken the time to ask questions and to listen carefully. Learn this skill early on, and you can avoid making these typical and very unnecessary errors.

13

Be open and approachable

1. **Decide at the outset of your working life that you will be open and approachable.**

   Even if this has not been easy for you in your life to date, resolve to be approachable in your working life. This will stand to you for the next forty years or as long as you remain in the workforce.

2. **Maintain a friendly appearance.**

   If this does not come naturally to you, at least avoid presenting an unfriendly and forbidding appearance. Work is challenging enough without people presenting themselves in such an off-putting manner.

3. **Accept that most people naturally gravitate towards people who appear warm and friendly.**

   It is a fact of human nature that this is the case, and it is a definite plus if you can present yourself in this light. Even if this is difficult for you initially, it is worth persisting as it is fundamental to being successful at work. This kind of demeanour will help you to become a go-to person, which I will address in Section 42.

4. **Smile.**

   The simple act of smiling goes a long way to making someone appear approachable. Some people find this does not come easily to them, especially in a work situation. However, as work is going to be such a big part of your life for most of your life, it is worth making an effort to present a friendly appearance.

5. **Accept that there will be days when you will not feel either open or approachable.**

   That will not go against you if you are normally approachable. No one expects anyone to be cheerful all of the time as life is not as simple as that.

6. **Do not complain that being friendly shouldn't matter so much.**

   I have known many employees over the years who found this aspect of work difficult. They considered it unfair that people of a friendly disposition tended to advance more quickly or progress further than they did. Remember, all things being equal, people like to deal with people they like. As you are not going to be able to change this reality of human nature, try to accept it and adapt to it as best you can.

7. **Adopt a business-like posture.**

   People are more likely to approach work colleagues who have an alert and business-like posture. Equally so, people are less likely to approach colleagues who are slumped over the desk or who appear to be bored or disinterested.

8. **Be flexible and go the extra mile for people who do approach you.**

   If you acquire this kind of reputation, people will not be as easily deterred even if you do not appear particularly open or approachable.

Summary:

Decide at the outset that you will make an effort to be open and approachable, and you will quickly become known for having these qualities. As well as making your time at work more enjoyable, this will improve your chances of being considered for internal promotion because these qualities are even more important at the senior manager level within most organisations. Maintain a business-like posture and always be flexible and willing to go the extra mile.

14

Adopt a positive approach

1. **Try to be positive in your approach at all times.**

   As per the previous section, most employees tend to gravitate towards approachable people, and such people are usually positive. If you are a naturally upbeat person, this may come easily to you, but even if you are quiet and reserved by nature, you must try to display a positive approach from the start of your working life. It will make your life at work so much easier.

2. **Develop a positive expectation of the resolution of any issue which arises at work.**

   This will ensure that you bring energy and enthusiasm to the resolution of the problem, motivating other people who may also be working on this problem.

3. **Take a negative response positively.**

   Taking this to mean 'not now' rather than 'never' is a good attitude and will put you on the way to developing a positive profile. Obviously, there are times when 'No' definitely means 'No,' but it is usually clear when that is the case.

4. **Communicate positivity by being energetic and enthusiastic.**

   This is particularly important when you are making a presentation where you are trying to persuade others to take some course of action.

5. **Communicate with the positive expectation of a successful outcome to what you are proposing.**

   This is essential if you want to get your proposal approved. I realise that it can be much more difficult to propose projects if you have to make your proposal via Zoom as this is not an ideal medium for 'selling' an idea.

6. **Start the day with a positive and upbeat approach.**

   This will not only get your day off to a good start, but it will also have a knock-on effect on your colleagues within your department and across the company. It will be particularly important that you have this approach if you have any dealings with customers. The need for positivity was never more evident than during the global COVID-19 pandemic and it is likely to be needed under the hybrid working model.

7. **Use positive language and action verbs to generate positive momentum among those you are working with.**

   This may not be your natural style, but you must develop it to a certain level, or you will struggle to be heard, especially if there are more persuasive employees within your group. While it is not easy to generate huge enthusiasm if you are not naturally that way, it should be easier to adopt the language of business. This invariably involves action verbs and an absence of vague and imprecise words that can easily create doubt among your audience.

8. **Try to surround yourself with positive people at work and in your private life as far as possible.**

   Not only will this mean that you won't have the energy drained out of you by negative people, but you will get a lift from these upbeat people if your energy levels dip which will occasionally happen to even the most positive people.

9. **Watch uplifting programmes and read positive news stories in your personal time.**

These can all help to boost your positivity, whereas disheartening programmes and stories can dampen your enthusiasm and can even be depressing at times. Watching or listening to too much news about COVID-19 was an example of something that could drag down even the most positive people.

10. **Be disciplined in your use of social media.**

It is easy to spend a lot of time on social media as it is a very addictive habit. It is also easy to be adversely affected by some social media content. Be vigilant about the amount of time you spend on social media, the sites you use, and the content you read so that it does not negatively influence you.

Summary:

By adopting a positive approach to your work from day one, you will get your working life off to a good start. Having positive expectations when presented with a problem or when making a presentation increases your chances of a successful outcome. Associating with positive people will also help you to maintain a positive approach, especially in trying times. Be careful what programmes you watch or listen to, and be particularly vigilant in your use of social media.

15

Learn to read your boss

1. **Learn to read people, especially your boss.**

   One of the things you will have to become competent at if you are to succeed at work is to be able to read people. The first person that you should take the time to understand is your manager, i.e. your boss.

2. **Study their body language and their modus operandi and try to detect a pattern of behaviour.**

   You will need to learn to recognise when it is a good time to approach them. Are they much the same all day, are they generally calm, or do they tend to get flustered easily? Do they prefer written communications or face-to-face meetings? Do they take the time to chat, or are they brief and to the point? Accept that it may take time to learn to read your boss as you will be preoccupied with your thoughts and emotions as you settle into your new job.

3. **Develop some competence in this ability for short-term and long-term advancement.**

   If you are a person with a technical qualification, this kind of thing may not come easily to you, especially if it is something you are not naturally interested in. However, you need to understand that a failure to do so could easily inhibit your effectiveness in your new role, or at the very least, it could reduce your chances of advancement within the company, or within other companies you may subsequently move to.

Some technical people take the view that this is very unfair as an ability to read people is not what they signed up for. That may be the case, but an ability to read people is essential, especially if you are interested in progressing into a management role. Some basic competence in this area is increasingly being considered essential in most professional roles in business.

4. **Ask your colleagues for guidance if necessary.**

Experienced colleagues will often be able to advise you on these kinds of things. They have been there for some time and 'know the ropes,' enabling them to accurately detect the signals.

5. **Study emails sent to you by your boss, and you will readily be able to establish their written communication style.**

If your boss is brief and to the point, you should adopt a similar style. As we know from the section on time management, time and attention span are in short supply. Even if your boss is not brief in their correspondence, it is generally better to get to the point quickly and to try to express yourself succinctly. You may struggle with this for a while, as written communications at work may be quite different from what you were used to at college.

6. **Ask their P.A., if they have one, as you can be sure that person has become very skilled at reading their boss.**

If you can establish a friendly or even a cordial relationship with them, they will be able to read the cues for you. Much of this kind of thing falls under the heading of developing 'cop on,' which you may imagine would be very common, but, unfortunately, that is often not the case with recently qualified professionals.

Summary:

Reading your boss, or 'boss management' as some may cynically call it, is an important skill even though you may reasonably point out that it is not one you signed up for. However, it is a skill you will need to acquire some level of competence in, especially as you are likely to have many different types of bosses with very different personalities over the course of your working life.

16

Be flexible

1. **Learn to be flexible.**

   This is another attribute that I strongly recommend you add to your list of essential personal qualities. Interestingly, IDA-Ireland (Irish Development Agency) cites the flexibility of the Irish workforce as one of the main reasons that Ireland has been so successful at attracting multinational companies into Ireland. It is also why so many of these companies have significantly expanded their operations in Ireland, well in excess of the size they had originally projected.

2. **Be flexible to ensure you can work effectively with colleagues and clients.**

   Research clearly indicates that businesspeople naturally gravitate towards someone who adopts a flexible approach as opposed to someone who is rigid in their thinking.

3. **Be flexible in any project team you participate in to contribute to the effectiveness of the team.**

   If you are flexible, colleagues will be keen to work on projects with you and your boss will recognise you as someone they can count on to be reasonable in your approach. Other managers may also notice your approach and try to get you to join their team or ask your boss to assign you to a cross-functional project team.

Note: I would not recommend a change of permanent role in the first year of your employment as you have much to learn within your current department before you decide to move to another.

4. **Be flexible in all aspects of your work.**

    This should include your starting and finishing times, coffee break, and lunch break times, your willingness to juggle your schedule to take on a project that your boss needs to prioritise, your willingness to help a colleague on some issue they are struggling with, or your modus operandi generally. Your flexibility will be noted, and you will be identified as a person with a positive attitude to their job and to their employer.

5. **Understand that this flexibility will be noted in performance management reviews and succession planning meetings.**

    Such flexibility is a necessary attribute when considering someone for a significant salary increase and promotion. The presence of flexibility becomes increasingly important as a person advances in an organisation.

6. **Recognise that if you have some interface with customers, they will greatly appreciate your flexible approach.**

    Such an approach by you is likely to improve the relationship between your employer and the customer. It may also make it more likely that the customer may express an interest to your manager in working with you again, should the need arise. As mentioned in Section 43, this experience of customer interface will help to broaden your business perspective.

7. **Be flexible in adopting others' preferences regarding the time, venue and format of meetings.**

   Such flexibility will be noted and appreciated. Similarly, volunteering to take the minutes of a meeting and circulating them promptly are other ways of displaying flexibility.

8. **Do not let people take advantage of your flexibility.**

   This means that you should avoid taking on tasks that are too far removed from the responsibilities of your role and will be of no benefit to you. They may even take away from your performance in your present job.

Summary:

This is an approach I recommend you adopt from day one. It is a much sought-after quality in any professional and will stand to you in your first job and throughout your working life. Flexibility is widely considered to be an essential quality in anyone with aspirations for a management position.

17

Adopt a problem-solving approach

1. **Be prepared to present a possible solution to a problem when you bring it to your boss's attention.**

   In most situations, it would be considered unacceptable for a professional to bring a problem to their boss's attention without considering possible solutions. This is particularly true if it is your responsibility to solve the problem. It is also true if your input is likely to be part of the solution and you can resolve the problem in your own department.

2. **Try to solve a problem as closely as possible to the level where it arises.**

   This is a good general rule relating to solving problems, especially those that can be solved in your own department without having to take up your boss's time. I remember a grumpy manager, having been presented with a routine problem, saying to an unfortunate subordinate one day, "Why should I keep a dog if I have to do my own barking?" Not very subtle, but the point about not involving your boss unless necessary is very valid.

3. **Adopt this policy in your interactions with other departments.**

   Again, this all calls for judgment, and this judgment only comes with experience. Because of this, most companies and managers are usually very understanding of newly-qualified professionals looking for considerable direction in the early part of their working life.

4. **Show initiative and adopt a problem-solving approach to enhance your reputation within the company.**

   This will be seen to maximum effect if you are also seen to be an effective communicator in your oral and written communications.

5. **Acquire a reputation as a problem-solver and be noted as a person who is generally seen as part of the solution rather than as part of the problem.**

   People are quickly categorised in this way. Those who are consistently seen as part of the problem often have a short tenure in a well-run business. This is understandable as any company can recruit people who are good at identifying problems, but that is only half the battle. Companies really want to recruit professional employees who can identify a problem but can also come up with one or more possible solutions to that problem.

Summary:

Do not bring a problem to your boss's attention unless this is necessary. If you do have to do so, please also be prepared to suggest possible solutions to the problem, so you are seen as a professional with a problem-solving approach.

18
Do not take things personally

1. **Learn not to take things personally.**

   In offering this advice, I know how difficult it is to follow it having fallen into this trap several times myself over the years. It is very easy to over-identify with your work and personal work projects, and take it personally if they come in for criticism. It is human nature to feel overprotective in this area. It isn't always easy to regard criticism as being professional and constructive as opposed to it being personal and destructive.

2. **Try to view your critic as someone doing their job.**

   As previously covered, organisations are set up with checks and balances to ensure that proposals, particularly expensive and time-consuming ones, are closely examined by several people before a decision is made to proceed with or drop a proposal.

   By adopting this approach, you will hopefully be open to taking criticism on board by seeing some merit in it and improving your original idea or proposal. You will also be seen to be mature by being open to criticism early in your career, especially when you have invested a lot of time and effort in formulating a proposal or fine-tuning a presentation.

3. **Remember your proposal may have merit, but it may have been presented poorly.**

I have often seen a proposal that was initially rejected being subsequently accepted. This happened because the presenter had the maturity to be open to present their case again, in a more compelling manner. In these cases, the presenter took the time to ask each of their critics for specific feedback on their presentation. They often found that people actually saw some merit in their proposal but found it was not presented persuasively or was presented in an unsuitable format.

4. **Differentiate between professional criticism and personal criticism.**

You must learn to make this distinction as soon as possible. The former is part of the job, and the second most definitely isn't. It is unprofessional and potentially destructive, but it does happen occasionally. If it does, all you can do is walk away and leave the matter for the time being. Hopefully, the person will think better of their outburst and subsequently apologise. Otherwise, you could decide to approach them again or email them to ascertain what exactly is their problem with your proposal. If you continue to experience hostility, you should advise the other party that you will have to report their behaviour to your manager or to HR.

5. **Do not retaliate in response to personal criticism, as it will only escalate matters further.**

You need to remember that if you retaliate, you will be seen as part of the problem even if you didn't cause it in the first instance. As per the previous point, if the problem persists, you should report it through the appropriate channels.

6. **Run your idea past your boss or a colleague before presenting it at a meeting.**

   You can significantly reduce the risk of criticism at a meeting if you present your idea to your boss or a colleague before formally presenting it.

7. **Run your ideas by other stakeholders if necessary.**

   If the idea has the support of your boss and departmental colleagues, it is time to run it past other stakeholders. Before you formally present it, take on board any comments or suggestions you consider appropriate and incorporate them into your presentation. As well as getting some useful feedback, this approach should prevent a lot of unnecessary embarrassment which might arise if your proposal was heavily criticised in a public forum.

Summary:

It is imperative that you learn to distinguish between criticism of your idea and criticism of you as a person. You should be open to all constructive criticism that could enhance and improve your proposal. The earlier you can do this, the earlier you will mark yourself down as a mature person willing to accept constructive feedback. Follow the advice outlined earlier if you are subjected to personal criticism.

19

Display initiative and judgment

1. **Develop a reputation of being someone who uses their initiative and knows when such initiative is called for.**

   It is tempting for you as a willing new graduate to use your initiative, but it is important to learn to identify a situation where using your initiative is inappropriate and where your manager or some more experienced professional or executive has to be consulted. This type of judgment only comes after a certain amount of trial and error. Be careful not to show too much initiative until your judgment becomes more reliable.

2. **Be patient with yourself in developing the judgment to know when initiative is called for.**

   This judgment only comes with experience. Unfortunately, this realisation often only dawns after a young professional makes a call on something where they did not have sufficient experience to make that call. Some companies and bosses are good at encouraging initiative and accepting the risk involved, but others are not. You need to understand your manager's expectations regarding the appropriate use of your initiative as a newly appointed professional.

3. **Show initiative in line with your level of expertise.**

   A good example of a situation where you need to show initiative is when you complete a project when your manager is in a meeting and you are at a loose end as to what to do next. Look at your objectives and start working on one of these rather than sitting around waiting for your manager to emerge from the meeting. Even if your manager decides you should work on a different and more important task, they will be pleased you took the initiative to start working on another task rather than sitting around doing nothing.

4. **Never allow yourself to be pressured into taking the initiative beyond your level of expertise.**

   If a situation arises when your boss is on annual leave, and you are asked to make a decision on something in your area of expertise, but beyond your level of competence, you need the judgment to realise that this not a situation where you should decide to display initiative. Unfortunately, some young professionals can be encouraged or even pressured into taking the initiative in such a situation, and when this happens, it invariably ends badly.

5. **Do not ask for guidance on the same type of issue more than once, twice at most.**

   If you pay attention the first time you ask for this type of guidance, you should be able to apply it in a similar situation. If necessary, take notes that you can refer to if you do not fully remember the required procedure.

6. **Work as hard when your manager is out of the office as you would when they are in.**

   If you know your manager will be away for a while and you are unsure what the next project you should be working on is even after applying the 80/20 rule, then look for direction before they go away. If the remaining objectives are of equal or similar importance, then use your initiative to decide which project to prioritise. It is a poor reflection of a professional if they do not work as diligently when their boss is absent as when they are present.

7. **Display initiative when you are on top of your work.**

If a new project arises which requires a member from your team, this may be a time to show initiative and volunteer, especially if it is a short-duration project which will not occupy you for long. If a longer-term project arises that you are interested in, then ask your manager's permission before volunteering to be part of the team.

Summary:

Using your initiative is another of the qualities you should look to display in your first job. The challenge for you is to learn as quickly as possible to exercise this initiative at the appropriate time. You may sometimes make the wrong decision, but unless this indicates very poor judgment and has very adverse consequences, most companies will back you for showing your initiative.

20

Develop a reputation as a team player

1. Decide to be seen as a team player from day one.

Being a team player will make your working life much easier than if you are seen as a loner, nerd, snob, or any other reason a person may have for taking a solitary approach. Being a team player is a much sought-after quality in employees, and I would strongly encourage you to be seen as one in your interactions with your fellow employees. As well as it being pragmatic to get on with your fellow employees, it also makes work much more enjoyable and fulfilling if you enjoy working with your colleagues and being part of a team. I would advocate that you adopt a similar approach with suppliers and customers.

2. Implement the team-player approach in the company as a whole.

Of course, you should try to be a team player within your department, but if you limit your definition of a team to only apply to your department, you are defining yourself much too narrowly. Such a narrow definition of the concept of being a team player may limit your success with your first employer but also with future employers if you do not learn to adopt a broader approach to this matter. You also run the risk of contributing to an 'us and them' thought process within your department, which means you would be missing out on the necessary interconnectedness of all employees within an organisation. This narrow definition of a team player, where you limit it to your current department, is a mistake I have seen many people make. As discussed earlier, only associating with people from your own background or your own age group greatly limits your range of experiences at work. I would argue strongly that it also reduces your potential influence within the company as a whole.

3. **Being a team player means there is great synergy in a department or in the organisation as a whole.**

   This can result in exceptional levels of productivity, quality, innovation, and customer service. This is very much as it should be where an organisation is much more than just the sum of its parts. To fully avail of these synergies, I would encourage you to become a team player in its broadest sense from day one.

4. **Being a team player doesn't mean you are exempt from making hard decisions that may put you in an uncomfortable position with other team members.**

   As covered in the previous section, even a team player has to deal with challenging situations which may cause you to feel conflicted in trying to resolve them. I would suggest your prime influence in such situations must be defined by the needs of the business for openness and transparency rather than by narrow departmental considerations. It is ultimately to the advantage of the team and its members that they adopt a similar approach rather than trying to cover up errors within the department, however tempting that option may be in the short term.

5. **Share the credit where your work on a project receives positive recognition.**

   In this situation, while taking your share of any well-deserved recognition, you should generously give credit to others who may have contributed in any way to your success or to the success of a project where your role was more evident. Failure to share credit means you run the risk of being seen as being selfish, self-centred and not a real team player. This can also have the effect of you being given minimal support in future projects because of your lack of respect for your fellow team members.

6. **Acknowledge when you make a mistake that impacts your team or the company as a whole.**

   As per the previous section, never try to cover up your mistake or attempt to spread the blame to others who are not culpable. Any failure on your part to be upfront about your errors will be seen negatively by your manager, colleagues, and across the company.

7. **Make an effort to draw attention to a colleague's good performance if you feel it has been overlooked.**

   You can do this by acknowledging it to the person concerned and bringing it to the attention of the relevant department manager. That is what a good team player would do in that kind of scenario.

Summary:

From day one, decide to be a team player within your department and within the company as a whole. Be generous in giving credit to others where this is deserved. Accept your share of the blame where this is warranted. Always take the long-term view in difficult situations and try to influence others to take a similar approach.

21

Adopt a policy of 'no surprises'

1. **Adopt this policy from day one because it has been my experience that most bosses do not like surprises.**

   Surprises at work are, more often than not, unpleasant. This is because they usually involve someone withholding information to the point that a situation that may have been readily dealt with had it been known about earlier, has now escalated into a crisis.

2. **Tell your boss immediately if you made an error that will impact a project your department is working on.**

   As I have pointed out, you may be reluctant to approach your boss to admit your error because you may fear their reaction. However, you have to overcome this natural reluctance immediately because otherwise, the matter could escalate into something that could become very serious for you, your boss, their boss, and potentially, in a worst-case scenario, for the company as a whole. If you fail to tell your boss immediately, you deprive them of the opportunity to resolve the problem at the earliest opportunity. In the case of a very serious error, where your failure to advise your boss on time results in them being disciplined or having their employment terminated, your employment will probably be terminated as well.

3. **Advise whether you can rectify the error.**

   If you think you will need assistance from the boss or a senior member of the project team to rectify the error, you need to request this assistance immediately.

4. **Indicate the timeframe to resolve the problem if you know how long this will take.**

    However, do not underestimate the likely time involved in the hope of appeasing your boss because a failure to rectify the problem in the proposed timeframe will only make a bad situation much worse.

5. **Don't ever try to hide your error because that will make matters much worse when it is discovered.**

    If you decide to hide an error, you will deprive your boss or the project team of the chance to correct the error as soon as possible, and you may significantly add to the costs ensuing from the error. More importantly, by concealing your error, you will raise questions not just about your technical competence but also about your integrity. The latter could well result in your employment being terminated.

6. **Don't try to the blame someone else for your error.**

    You are most likely to be found out if you do this, but even if you somehow get away with it, this will probably lead to a fundamental breach of trust between you and a team member. It may also give rise to some serious suspicions in your boss about you and your trustworthiness.

7. **Decide early on if you are clear that you have made a bad choice in accepting the job with your current employer.**

    If you are clear about this and have given the job and the company a chance, you are better to call it rather than be unhappy at work and have the company invest more time and money in training and developing you. These things happen, and it is much better that you call it before it becomes obvious to your boss and the decision is made for you.

Summary:

It is critically important that you appreciate bosses do not like surprises as they are invariably unpleasant. If you make a serious error, immediate honesty is your best and only policy if you hope to have a future with that employer. If you can solve or help to solve the problem, apply yourself diligently to this task. Never try to blame anyone else for your error.

22

Attend to your physical and mental wellbeing

A. Physical Fitness

1. **Attain and maintain a high level of physical fitness.**

    In today's fast-paced world of higher customer expectations, greater company demands on employees, and higher levels of competition, your physical fitness is more important than ever. Without this physical fitness, you may find it difficult to have the stamina to keep up with the demands of business today.

2. **Choose a physical fitness programme that best suits your needs and one that you are willing to commit to fully.**

    There are a wide range of programmes available nowadays, so it should be possible to find a programme that best suits your needs. Suitable programmes should address all aspects of physical fitness – cardiovascular endurance, muscular strength and endurance, flexibility, and body fat composition.

3. **Try to build some variety into your fitness regime so that it doesn't become tedious.**

    This is important because if boredom sets in, this may cause you to discontinue the programme or be less vigilant in adhering to it.

4. **Make limited use of gym facilities provided by your employer.**

   Ostensibly, these may seem attractive as they can make it easy for employees to achieve and maintain a high level of fitness. While I acknowledge the attraction of having such facilities available to you at work, I have some reservations about the trend for companies to provide gym facilities. I recommend that you consciously try to create a division between your work life and your personal life. It may be better for you to exercise elsewhere at least some of the time to facilitate this separation.

Summary:

In my opinion, the demands of business make physical fitness essential for a person embarking on what may be a forty-year working life. Because achieving and maintaining physical fitness requires great willpower and determination, it is important that you adopt a fitness programme that you find interesting and are willing to commit to on a long-term basis.

B. Mental Wellbeing

1. **Pay at least as much attention to your mental health as to your physical health.**

   Thankfully, the importance of mental health is much better understood and appreciated than when I commenced my working life. It is encouraging that the issue of mental health was really highlighted during the COVID-19 pandemic, where most people worked from home over a protracted period.

2. **Identify someone to talk to about your mental health if you are experiencing psychological problems.**

   This can be your partner, a family member, a friend, your boss, someone in HR, or if you need professional input, a counsellor, a doctor, or some combination of these resources. It is generally accepted that women are much better at talking about their feelings, but thankfully, there is a growing tendency for men to look for support when they need it.

3. **Attend to your physical health to help your mental health.**

   Physical fitness can help reduce three mental health conditions that are becoming increasingly prevalent in today's fast-paced world, i.e. anxiety, depression, and stress. Physical health also helps with self-esteem, sleep, and resilience.

4. **Participate in company wellness programmes.**

   Many companies nowadays have excellent wellness programmes. If your company has such a programme, it would be advisable to check this out as there may be many activities in it which could help you to develop your overall wellbeing. Such programmes can also involve some team-building activities which can make your work experience more rewarding.

5. **Consider practicing meditation and mindfulness.**

   If you can find or make the time in your daily schedule for meditation, this could significantly improve your mental health by helping to make you calm and give you more insight into your life overall. If you decide to meditate, I suggest you do so at the same time every day, as this will increase your chances of adhering to your meditation practice. If you cannot fit in a meditation programme, I recommend that you learn to make a few minutes every day to be more mindful at work, as this can provide you with much-needed moments of calm in your otherwise busy day.

Summary:

I strongly recommend that you prioritise your mental health at work and give it at least as much attention as your mental health outside of work and as much attention as you do to your physical health. This attention will help you in your first job and your entire working life as you go through different stages in your life. Work is much more stressful nowadays and because of this, taking care of one's mental health has to be treated as a priority by you and all employees.

23
Maintain a healthy diet

1. **Boost your physical and mental wellbeing by having a healthy diet.**

   This follows naturally from the previous point. It is widely accepted nowadays that physical and mental health programmes will be much more successful if they are supported by a healthy diet. There is also general agreement nowadays as to what foods are nutritional and what foods are regarded as junk foods. If you are in any doubt about any aspect of this, there is comprehensive information on nutritional and junk foods freely available online.

2. **Get your day off to a good start with a healthy breakfast.**

   It is widely accepted that a healthy breakfast helps control your weight and blood sugar level, and it gives you vitamins and minerals that make you feel well and think clearly. For example, oatmeal gives you carbohydrate and fibre to help you maintain an ideal level of bacteria in your gut and the fruit gives you fibre and vitamins.

3. **Try to stick to three main meals in the day.**

   Avoid eating between meals even if there is a canteen at work with many tasty snacks that could put paid to your best intentions.

4. **Try to eat a light lunch.**

   Eating too much at lunchtime, particularly if you include some poor food choices, can make you sluggish in the afternoon. Try to eat a lunch that is nutritionally balanced and enjoyable. For example, for a balanced lunch, try to include items from three of the following food groups – fruits, grains, protein, and dairy.

5. **Try to eat a balanced main meal in the evening.**

Select foods that you enjoy that will keep you satiated and leave you less likely to reach for a late-night snack. An ideal dinner features a balance of vegetables, proteins, grains, and healthy fat. For example, grilled salmon, roasted vegetables, and brown rice.

6. **Try not to eat after your dinner.**

It is generally agreed that it is better for a person's digestive system not to eat after 7.00 p.m. in the evening. This may be difficult at times but if you do eat late in the evening, try to do so on an exceptional basis. Eating late at night can also interfere with your sleep pattern, which can leave you short of energy if you have to work the following day.

7. **Be aware of foods you would be better to avoid or to take in moderation.**

Some examples are French fries, sugary drinks, chocolate bars, white bread, fruit juices, pastries, buns and cakes, ice cream. Some of these are very tasty and very tempting, but they have limited nutritional value. I have succumbed to many of these over the years and still do occasionally, so I appreciate how difficult it is to moderate one's intake of such foods but also how important this is. Thankfully, there is much greater awareness of the importance of nutrition these days, and hopefully, as a result of this, you will have already established a healthy diet.

8. Be aware of nutritional foods that you may be allergic to.

Gluten, some dairy products, yeast, and certain nuts are some examples of these. It is worth having an allergy test done if you think that this point has relevance for you.

9. Go easy on the alcohol.

Alcohol in moderation is fine, as alcohol plays an important part in many people's social lives. 'Moderation' is the apt word as alcohol abuse has ruined many people's lives and careers. If you have to work the next day, I strongly advise you not to drink, even in moderation.

Summary:

A balanced diet can support your physical and mental health regimes, whereas an unbalanced diet can seriously undermine them. There is a general consensus nowadays as to which foods and drinks provide the highest nutritional content. You will need to be very disciplined to limit your intake of foods with little or no nutritional value as they are often attractively packaged, tasty, and heavily promoted.

24

Achieve and exceed your goals and objectives

You have been hired to achieve certain goals and objectives, and it is critical that you are made aware of these and become focused on them as soon as possible after you commence your first job or, indeed, any subsequent job.

1. **Be very clear of the specific goals and objectives of your position.**

   The earlier you are aware of these goals and objectives, the better. Usually, an outline of the duties and responsibilities of your job is contained in the job description for that position. In most well-managed businesses, you will also be provided with a list of goals and objectives within a month of your start date.

2. **Ask for a list of goals and objectives if you are not given these within four weeks.**

   I fully appreciate that as a person new to the workforce, you may be reluctant to do this but if you do not, you may be working away under the illusion that you are doing a good job based on your understanding of the role. However, should your manager have a different understanding of the key requirements of the position, you will be the person who will bear the brunt of this misunderstanding, even though it was clearly your manager's responsibility to provide you with a list of goals and objectives.

3. **Remember, as a new employee, you are on probation (probably for six months).**

    This means that it is important that you are proactive in ensuring you know precisely what is expected of you and in what timeframe. As I have said already, you should not have to do this as it is clearly your manager's responsibility to do so. However, if your manager does not furnish you with your goals and objectives, you must look for the information so that you complete your probationary period satisfactorily.

4. **Clear up any ambiguity if there is any in your list of goals and objectives.**

    If you are unclear about the meaning of any of these or are unsure how you should achieve a particular goal, it is imperative that you raise this with your manager and ask for clarity or direction as the case may be. If you fail to do this, your manager will assume you know what is required of you and expect all of the goals and objectives to be met in the outlined timeframe.

    Ideally, the manager will ensure that you fully understand what is involved in achieving each objective, but if they do not, you must be proactive and ensure you fully understand what is expected of you.

5. **Look for a complete job description and a list of goals and objectives if you take up a newly created role.**

    If you have been recruited to fill such a role and have only been given bullet points for the position's duties, you should look for a complete job description and a list of goals and objectives pertaining to the role. If you are not supplied with these after requesting them, then write down your understanding of the role and the relevant goals and objectives and ask your manager to review, approve or modify these as the case may be.

6. **Look for KPIs (Key Performance Indicators) if you are in a position where objectives can be outlined in quantifiable terms.**

These indicators may be percentages, time frames, or monetary amounts. You need absolute clarity about these. Most companies will use these for roles where performance can be easily measured and quantified. It is in your interest to be fully aware of these metrics as it removes the potential for disagreement about what constitutes good or bad performance.

7. **Look for clarity as to what is expected of you if you are in a staffing role where metrics cannot be readily applied.**

Setting objectives and measuring performance is not as easy in staffing roles. However, it is still important that there is a clear understanding between you and your manager as to what constitutes satisfactory performance.

A good question to ask of your boss in such a position is, "What would success look like after the completion of my probationary period?" In a role without any metrics, it is incumbent on you to clearly understand what exactly is expected of you, in what time frame, and to what standard. Without this clarity, there will only be one loser when it comes to performance review time. At that time, it will not do you any good to point out that you were not given clarity as to what was expected of you, even if you had requested this information.

8. **Ascertain if there is room for negotiation on a particular goal or objective if you think it is unrealistic.**

   If you genuinely believe an objective cannot be achieved to the standard required or in the time frame specified, you should try to renegotiate the point of contention. Good managers will usually be open to negotiation within reason. You should raise any goal with your manager that you consider unachievable. Unless you raise this as an issue, your manager is entitled to assume that you see the goals and objectives as achievable and will judge you accordingly.

Summary:

Most well-run companies are good at providing job descriptions, goals, objectives, and KPIs, but if they fail to do so, then you must be proactive in getting the information you require. If any goal seems unrealistic to you, then you should put forward a strong case to get an unrealistic objective modified. You may think this is a lot to ask of a new employee, and I agree with that observation. However, I recommend you be proactive if you are not provided with clear and realistic goals and objectives. Failure to do so could result in you being found to have not completed your probationary period satisfactorily. As a result you will most likely be let go which will put a damaging blemish on your employment record.

25

Achieve and exceed your budgets and KPIs

1. Commit yourself to achieve or, preferably, exceed your KPIs.

For example, if you are in a sales role, you are most likely to have a sales budget. As a junior sales representative, you are likely to have a lower budget than a more senior salesperson. This reflects your lack of prior sales experience and your absence of previous work experience. Most junior sales roles have relatively modest sales budgets. Achieving them is the bare minimum that is likely to be acceptable to your manager.

I recommend that you should always aim to exceed your targets and KPIs rather than just meet them. By doing this, you start to make your mark in the company and begin to acquire a reputation as a high performer, as someone who is ambitious and wants to progress within the company.

2. Aim to achieve/exceed any other metrics in your objectives.

These could include reducing costs, achieving some target by a certain date, or improving efficiencies. These are targets you should also seek to exceed for the reasons outlined in the previous point.

3. Exceed your targets to positively influence your performance review discussions.

This should mean you will pass your probationary period provided you have discharged the other duties and responsibilities of your position. It should also improve your prospects of getting a decent salary increase when that falls due for review.

4. **Propose a relevant metric or brainstorm with your boss if you are given an objective without a metric assigned to it.**

   This should work in your favour as it will provide you with another opportunity to be seen as a proactive employee and a 'highflyer' within the company.

5. **Ensure you never interfere with the prospects of one of your colleagues achieving their objectives.**

   No matter how successful you are, do not fall into the trap of some highflyers and get a reputation for taking shortcuts. If this causes you to interfere with someone else's role performance, you run the risk of being perceived as a maverick. This is a reputation that is likely to interfere with your ambitions with your employer.

6. **Discharge the full responsibilities of your role by maintaining good working relationships with your colleagues.**

   Failure to work effectively with colleagues could mean you will not successfully complete your probationary period, making it even more important that you acquire a reputation of being a team player, as outlined in Section 20.

   Even if you come through your probationary period successfully, you will be kept under close review if you have rubbed some people up the wrong way in the first six months of your employment. It is important that you make every effort to work effectively with your colleagues.

Summary:

I strongly recommend you set out to at least meet, and preferably exceed, the objectives of your position. Provided you do this without falling out with colleagues and interfering with their work, you should acquire a reputation as a hard-working employee and a person with good promotional prospects within the company.

26

Learn to be resilient

1. **Be resilient or learn to be resilient.**

   All of the 50 qualities in this book are ones I consider necessary for you to succeed in your career, but if I were asked to pick my top three reasons why some people are more successful than others, resilience would be one of them. Regardless of what kind of organisation you join and how successful you are, it is inevitable that you will experience many setbacks along the way. It is your ability to cope with these setbacks that will determine the trajectory of your career.

2. **Build on the resilience that has got you to this point, where you have secured your first job.**

   You have shown resilience in getting through college and getting your first job, but your resilience will be subjected to much more intense and sustained scrutiny over the course of your working life. This will be particularly true if you are employed in a very demanding business and in a very competitive market sector.

3. **Certain company cultures require more resilience in employees.**

   An autocratic command and control organisation (there are still a few out there!) can be more hard-nosed and less tolerant of errors than a more consultative employer. Such a culture can require new employees to toughen up and develop resilience quickly if they are to survive in such an environment.

4. **Certain jobs require greater resilience than others. For example, those with stretching sales budgets.**

I ran a recruitment and HR consultancy for twenty-five years and have seen many employees who initially embarked on their careers with great energy and enthusiasm. However, some became discouraged if they failed to achieve their targets, even if that failure was due to circumstances outside of their control. For example, a vacancy was cancelled or the person they put forward for the job decided not to relocate. The mistake some professionals in these roles often made was that they took their failure to fill the job as a personal slight which reflected badly on them, whereas the more resilient individual was able to take such a setback in their stride and would immediately look for new positions to work on or look for additional candidates to put forward for the vacant position.

5. **Be resilient if you get negative feedback at a performance review.**

This is particularly important if you were under the impression you were performing well and were held in high regard, or you have never received this kind of feedback before. This setback can be particularly painful if it results in you receiving no salary increase or a minuscule increase. This could be discouraging and coping with the disappointment and disillusionment may call for considerable resilience on your part. Rather than sulk about this, my advice is to dust yourself down, make the necessary changes to get an improved rating in the company and a decent salary increase at the next salary review date.

6. **Develop resilience if you are repeatedly passed over for promotion.**

   You may need to have a very frank conversation with your boss to understand where you are falling short and what you have to do to rectify the situation. If you take on board your boss's feedback, this should help get your career back on track. If it doesn't, it may be time for you to consider working for a company where your skills will be recognised and rewarded better.

7. **Resilience may be required if you and your colleagues are under pressure because of quality issues in the department.**

   This can be difficult because it can be easy to feel that the spotlight is on you and your colleagues if such a scenario arises. It is also normal to feel the blame and disapproval of others in this kind of situation. You will need to be strong to avoid being discouraged and disillusioned by these feelings.

8. **Resilience may be required because of issues in your personal life that are causing you distress.**

   If this distress begins to impact your work performance, then speak to your boss or HR so that you can be 'cut some slack' in the short term while you resolve these personal matters. Most employers nowadays are better at dealing with these types of situations than they were in less-enlightened times.

Summary:

Work hard at developing your resilience. There are few qualities that you will need as much as resilience throughout your working life. Resilience is one of the character-building qualities that is essential for you to survive and thrive in a demanding work environment.

27

Be productive at meetings

1. **Learn early in your working life how to be effective at meetings.**

   If you are invited to a meeting, you need to prepare well for it. This means reviewing the agenda for the meeting and being ready to address any issues on the agenda where you may have an input. There is no excuse for going to a meeting unprepared, even if this is a widespread practice and something that can occur in numerous otherwise well-run businesses. If you are unsure of what is required of you at a meeting, ask the person who called the meeting what information they need so there is no ambiguity regarding what is expected of you.

2. **Pay attention at meetings.**

   It is easier to pay attention if it is a well-run meeting with an allocated time for each agenda item, than an open-ended meeting with no set time for each agenda item. If you have a relevant comment to make about someone else's agenda item, make your comment brief and to the point. If an issue drags on and only concerns you and one other attendee, offer to deal with it outside the meeting rather than waste other people's time.

3. **Address your agenda items succinctly, in a clear and decisive manner.**

   Ensure that what you are saying is clearly understood. If possible, anticipate any questions that may arise and be ready to address these.

4. **Speak to relevant parties before a meeting if an agenda item you are raising requires their support or some action from them.**

   If you cannot agree on the matter privately, you may both agree to discuss it at the meeting and get other people's input, or you may both decide to refer it to your boss or their boss as the issue may require their input.

5. **Consider whether or not to put an item on the meeting agenda if it involves some significant expenditure.**

   In this case it may be advisable to discuss it with your manager before the meeting and decide how best to progress the matter if they support it. Remember Section 21 about 'no surprises.'

6. **Recognise the difference between an agenda item which involves imparting some basic information and one requiring detailed discussion and a decision.**

   Attendees at meetings and chairpersons of meetings often fail to differentiate between the two and this can lead to the meeting losing direction, focus, and the attention of many of the participants. Meetings with agenda items that are likely to require much discussion, should be long enough to allow for a full discussion of each such agenda item. If you are proposing such an item for discussion, you need to ensure it is given adequate time on the agenda for the necessary discussion to take place.

7. **Avoid getting dragged into unproductive discussions at meetings.**

   In other words, do not be seen to be part of the problem at a meeting but be seen as part of the solution.

8. **Implement any action item assigned to you in a comprehensive manner as soon as possible after the meeting.**

   Ensure you address your action items fully and do not leave it until just before the next meeting to address any action item assigned to you. This is particularly important if there is a considerable amount of time between meetings.

9. **Adopt best practice if you are asked to chair a meeting.**

   You are unlikely to be asked to chair a meeting early in your career, but it can happen. If it does, ensure the meeting starts on time and stays on schedule. Be diplomatic but firm in ensuring that contributors stick to the agenda. Do not allow participants to drag out particular points or try to introduce additional items. Read out the agreed action items at the end of the meeting and publish the minutes as soon as possible afterwards.

Summary:

Meetings are an inevitable and integral part of life in a busy company. It is vitally important that you prepare well for every meeting you attend, contribute effectively and follow up promptly and comprehensively on any action items assigned to you. By conducting yourself in this manner, you will begin to build your profile as an effective employee and someone who could have a promising long-term future within the company.

28
Develop strong presentation skills

1. **Acquire this key competence as an essential part of your skillset.**
   This is imperative, especially in a large organisation where making presentations is an everyday event. Resolve to acquire this skill early in your career and look for opportunities to develop your competence by presenting your ideas in this format as often as possible.

2. **Recognise that most new employees find the thought of making a presentation to be very daunting.**
   In fact, the thought of making a presentation is regarded as one of most people's greatest fears. Do not worry if you feel apprehensive about making your first presentation or, indeed, subsequent presentations. Some level of anxiety is necessary to give your best in a presentation. Persist, even if it seems daunting, as proficiency in making presentations is a skill you must master if you are to progress in most large organisations.

3. **Think about what you want the audience to know or do after your presentation.**
   As well as being an important point in its own right, this is a good way of controlling your nerves. If you think more about what you want your audience to know or do, this will help take your mind off your own feelings about making the presentation.

4. **Do not concentrate all of your efforts on the content of the presentation.**

This is a typical rookie mistake. Obviously, the content has to be accurate and relevant but that alone doesn't guarantee the success of your presentation.

5. **Decide what medium to use and familiarise yourself with the technology involved before making your presentation.**

There is nothing more unsettling when commencing a presentation than to experience problems with the technology. It is also the quickest way to lose your audience's attention.

6. **Ensure charts are legible and use them sparingly.**

Use bullet points to highlight your key points. Charts should be seen as an aid to highlight key points, but they should not dominate your presentation.

7. **Avoid using too many charts or charts with too much information on them.**

This is a sure way to lose an audience, especially if there have been many presenters ahead of you. Use charts selectively to highlight your central message. Use bullet points to highlight important points. Charts are an aid to highlight the main points you wish to get across, but too many of them can readily dilute your central message. Remember, people are there to listen to you, you are the main visual aid, and they do not want to be subject to 'death by too many charts.'

8. **Try to use a format where the lights can remain on so you can maintain eye contact with your audience.**

   This will help you to see if your ideas are being understood. This issue of maintaining eye contact is crucial, and you need to become comfortable with it as quickly as possible. Do not turn your back on your audience to read your charts as you will lose eye contact with those present.

9. **Remember the importance of body language.**

   As well as eye contact, other aspects of body language are hand and facial gestures, posture, and body movement. All gestures should support your presentation, not take away from it in any way. Simple things like shuffling while standing, being self-conscious about your hands are all 'noise in the channel' and can distract your audience and take away from your presentation.

10. **Speak with conviction and enthusiasm.**

    You will have little chance of getting your proposals listened to and accepted if you present them in a monotone manner that lacks any energy. Do not speak all of the time. Pause to highlight key points and to give your audience a chance to consider these.

11. **Think about who your audience is.**

    If it is people in your own department, they will readily understand what you are talking about, but if it is people in another department such as finance, you need to talk in their language of costs, benefits, and return on investment.

12. Anticipate questions.

Many a good presentation has floundered because the presenter failed to anticipate an obvious question and then failed to answer it satisfactorily because of their lack of basic preparation.

13. Use humour selectively.

If you are a person who is comfortable with humour and can judge when the timing is right, then it is a great way of relaxing an audience and getting them on your side. This will usually have the knock-on benefit of relaxing you as well.

Summary:

You will need to acquire strong presentation skills if you wish to progress in your new job and career. As with other skills, identify people in the company who are skilled in this area and learn from them. Also, there are many excellent presenters on television, and you can learn a lot from studying them closely.

There are many points to master to become an effective presenter. If I were to highlight three, I would say maintain eye contact, speak with conviction and use charts sparingly.

One final point about preparations is that the key predictor of success in a presentation is the work done during the preparation stage. As Benjamin Franklin put it, 'By failing to prepare, you prepare to fail.'

29

Become an effective networker

A. Internal Networking

1. **Become an effective networker within your company.**
   Ideally, this skill is one you already have, and you will naturally apply it in your new job. However, if this is not one of your strengths, you will need to acquire a basic level of competence in this regard.

2. **Learn to be equally proficient in communicating with employees at all levels of the organisation.**
   I remember being surprised in my first position in industry at how many people struggled in this regard. This was probably because many new employees were used to being with their friends who typically were of a similar age and background. Some new employees could be unduly deferential to those in authority, and others were sometimes condescending to those they perceived to be in less important roles than themselves. The more successful networkers either didn't have this weakness in the first place, or if they did, they soon learned to overcome it and to mix comfortably with all fellow employees.

3. **Effective networkers are good at influencing employees and persuading them to take a course of action even though they may have no authority over them.**
   This is a form of personal power that can often be as effective or even more effective than positional power, especially

in companies with a relatively flat organisation structure. If you do not have this particular attribute, study others who have because you can learn a lot from them that will be of assistance to you throughout your career.

4. **Effective networkers are naturally comfortable with other people, and automatically take an interest in them.**

People tend to like people who take an interest in them, and as a result, they are more predisposed to assist them with a problem. Showing an interest in people may not come easily to you. It may feel somewhat contrived when you try to do it first, but if you can acquire some level of competence in this area, it will stand to you.

Summary:

If you are committed to realising your potential at work, you need to develop your internal networking skills. As a professional employee, you will need to be able to interact with employees at all levels of the organisation. This is one of the skills you must work on until you have required a basic level of competence. You may even find you come to like your colleagues more after a while!

B. External Networking

1. **Try to stay plugged into your personal network outside of the working environment.**

As a new employee, you will probably stay in contact with many of those in your personal network for a while. This will be easier if your first job is near your home but if it isn't, try to retain contact with your friends over weekends at home, so your world does not become overly influenced by your work and your work colleagues.

2. **Stay connected to some of those in the same profession or within your professional body.**

It is a short-sighted approach to disconnect from fellow professionals because you never know when you may need to tap into these networks. For instance, you may be made redundant at some stage in your career through no fault of your own and having a strong external network may be the route to your next job. Unfortunately, due to time pressures and often because some companies do not encourage external networking, many people make the mistake of not staying connected to their external network. In my case, I remained a member of the CIPD (Certified Institute of Personnel & Development) throughout my working life. I found it to be an essential part of my professional network.

Being affiliated to a professional body is also advantageous as such bodies usually run training programmes, seminars, workshops, and conferences, and many produce high-quality monthly publications. All of these can be beneficial for keeping current with the latest developments in your area of expertise. It is essential that you stay current in your profession as we are now in a world where information that may have been part of your degree is no longer seen as best practice a few short years afterwards.

Summary:

I recommend you keep connected to your external network throughout your working life. Limiting yourself to your internal network can leave you in a silo-like situation which is very limiting from a professional development point of view and could also be very harmful to you in the event of a redundancy scenario. This is particularly true if you stay a long time in the same company. Staying in touch with friends, or at least one or two old friends, can give you a broader perspective than if you only relate to current work colleagues. Stay affiliated with your relevant professional body for networking, information, and developmental purposes.

30
Establish a good timekeeping and attendance record

1. **Show you are a person your manager and colleagues can count on to be at work every day and be there on time.**

   Although this is a basic requirement of any job, I am highlighting it as it is not always adhered to, especially in some loosely managed organisations. You need to remember that as a new employee, you are on probation, and you should be at work on time every day as a poor record in this area could result in your being let go before or at the end of your probationary period. For a professional, being present and on time should be a prerequisite, but it is surprising how otherwise good performers can sometimes adopt a casual approach, especially in the area of timekeeping. As a new employee, you cannot afford to take liberties about your timekeeping and attendance regardless of whether your more experienced colleagues do so and even if your manager also has a casual approach to such matters.

2. **Be impeccable in this area as it is an indicator of a strong work ethic.**

   Even if your manager is not particularly vigilant in this area and your colleagues are casual about timekeeping and attendance, please do not adopt a similar approach as it is not in your best interests. Your current employer may tolerate such a casual approach, but many employers do not have such a liberal view of this matter. You should avoid slipping into bad practices in this area that you may have to correct if you move to another employer.

3. **Maintain good timekeeping standards, even if you work unpaid overtime.**

Many managers and professionals who do unpaid overtime have a relaxed attitude to being at work on time. I understand this attitude, but I disagree with it. I prefer to take the view that you should always be at work on time even if, as is likely, you also do some unpaid overtime. I recommend that you develop the habit of being on time as a matter of professional pride.

4. **Don't take 'duvet days.'**

This is a term that seems to have crept into modern parlance and indicates a very casual approach to taking the occasional day off work. I recently heard a chat show host on radio extolling the benefit of taking the occasional duvet day. I would strongly encourage you to ignore this kind of advice. You are paid to be at work every day you are fit to be there, and taking duvet days is most definitely not part of your contract of employment. The only exception to this advice would be where the company itself authorises the occasional day off as a way of showing appreciation for exceptional performance.

5. **Don't come to work if you are sick as this may extend your period of illness and affect other employees as well.**

Staying at home when you are sick has got nothing to do with taking a duvet day. If you go to work when you are ill, you could not only prolong your own illness, but you could also unintentionally pass on your illness to another employee. This would be irresponsible on your part. In my earlier working life, it was considered normal for employees to turn up for work when they would be quite ill. I did this myself on occasion. However, I am pleased that this kind of behaviour, however well-motivated, is no longer encouraged or even tolerated.

6. **Understand that some HR departments keep accurate attendance records and take them seriously.**

    Some companies are very vigilant in tracking time and attendance as they treat this issue seriously. Developing a record of casual absenteeism or of poor timekeeping could result in you failing to satisfactorily complete your probationary period which will likely affect you when you are going for another job.

7. **Being on time doesn't mean walking in the front door exactly at the official starting time.**

    Being on time means being at your desk at or before that time so that no time is lost unnecessarily going off for tea or coffee or settling down to a full-blown conversation about the night before. I realise this kind of work practice is the norm in certain organisations and institutions, but it is not the kind of behaviour that is likely to help further your career in a more progressive organisation.

8. **Be at your desk in good time so that you are mentally ready to start the day in an organised manner.**

    This is much more preferable than coming in late and being somewhat flustered, and then spending the rest of the day trying to catch up. Make it a habit to be at your desk in good time to avoid any unnecessary disruption at the start of your working day.

Summary:

This may seem like a basic requirement of any job, but it is not as widely practiced as you may expect. It is clear that some level of casual absenteeism and relaxed timekeeping have crept into some long-established organisations. I urge you to develop a reputation for always being at work unless you are genuinely ill. I would also encourage you to be punctual as a good record in both of these areas will stand to you throughout your working life.

31
Use the Performance Management System effectively

1. Adopt a positive approach to performance reviews.

As a new employee, you will be on probation for the first six months in most companies and even for the first twelve months in some organisations. During this time, you should expect to receive feedback on your performance from your manager.

2. Be proactive in looking for feedback.

If feedback from your manager is not forthcoming, ask for it. There is no point in complaining at the end of your probationary period that you got no feedback from your boss as it may be too late at that stage.

3. Continue to use performance review meetings effectively after completing your probationary period.

These are very important meetings in the context of your present role and in terms of your future with your current employer and subsequent employers.

4. Do not become sceptical about these reviews or view them as an ordeal undertaken to placate HR.

I can understand this scepticism but disagree strongly with it and would encourage you to look at these reviews more positively than many employees do. They present a rare opportunity for you to have your bosses undivided attention, to confirm how you are getting on in the company, and identify areas where your boss may feel you need to improve.

5. **Consider a performance review as an opportunity to discuss your progress and prospects with your boss.**

   You have the opportunity to express your ambitions within the company, to talk about your long-term career goals, and what steps you may need to take to achieve these goals.

6. **Consider a performance review as an opportunity to discuss your training and development needs.**

   This may involve company training programmes, relevant external training programmes, or possibly other formal education courses.

7. **Prepare well for performance reviews.**

   A performance review is a rare opportunity to find out how you are integrating into the company. It can also enable you to get a clear understanding of the opportunities your boss is considering for you, and how these align with your career goals.

   A performance review may be an opportunity for you to express an interest in moving laterally to another department to broaden your skillset and understanding of the company and its goals. Some professionals are not open to considering the advantages of a lateral move, but I disagree with this approach. In my opinion, a good lateral move has the potential to position you well for promotion in the future based on the broad skillset you have acquired. This is also an opportunity for you to discuss whether you wish to progress on a technical path or whether you see your long-term future in the area of management.

Note: As mentioned elsewhere, a lateral move is generally not recommended in one's first two years at work as there is so much to learn in your new role before considering moving laterally.

Summary:

This is an important part of your working life, and you need to treat it accordingly. I encourage you to ignore the widespread cynicism about performance reviews and look at them as an opportunity to gauge your progress, discuss your goals within the company, and clarify what you need to do to achieve these goals.

32

Adopt a policy of continuous improvement

1. **Adopt this policy from day one and continue to practice it throughout your career.**

   This is normal practice for ambitious employees who have a clear career path in mind and have the energy and determination to make their professional careers outstanding.

2. **This policy will ensure that you never become complacent.**

   It will ensure that you will seek to grow and develop incrementally as a professional on a daily basis. It is a very gradual process, like building a house brick by brick. You hardly notice it on a daily basis but when you look back over a year, you can see how much you have achieved.

3. **This policy will help you if you wish to become a go-to person within the company (see Section 42).**

   It almost goes without saying that anyone who aspires to be a go-to person in a department must have an ethos of continuous improvement about them. This is not a process of gradually acquiring knowledge almost by default just by being there on a daily basis. On the contrary, this is a deliberate and systematic way of building up a body of knowledge with the clear end goal of being an expert in your field.

4. Adopt this kind of approach to stand out.

By adopting this policy, you will quickly be seen as an ambitious employee who will soon begin to feature in your company's succession plan. This is very much how it works and is a process whereby the highflyers begin to stand out as exceptional employees because of their commitment to continuous improvement.

5. Try to associate as much as possible with employees with a similar philosophy of continuous improvement.

This often happens naturally as such people frequently seem to gravitate towards one another without consciously deciding to do so. The benefit of this happening is that these high-achievers feed off each other which adds momentum to the continuous improvement process. It also makes work feel like a process of flow rather than one of great effort for these much sought-after professionals.

6. Try to work for managers who also have a philosophy of continuous improvement.

Obviously, this won't always be possible, but if your manager is a high achiever themselves, this is a huge advantage as the standards they set and the momentum they generate will be particularly appreciated by those professionals with an ethos of continuous improvement.

7. Become an active member of a professional body and a person who embraces further professional education.

As per the previous section, this is a prerequisite for ambitious professionals who are determined to progress their careers systematically.

8. **Look to initiate product improvements, process improvements, or cost reductions.**

These are some of the ways for you to improve and to stand out from your colleagues. Your opportunity to stand out in this regard can be greatly enhanced if your employer operates a well-managed suggestion scheme. Such schemes are usually self-financing and provide a win/win opportunity for both employers and employees.

9. **Look for opportunities to participate in project teams.**

These may afford you the opportunity to improve your skillset. If possible, volunteer for challenging roles within the project team, which will stretch you even further.

10. **Only work for companies with a philosophy of continuous improvement.**

Many leading-edge companies have a clearly stated policy of continuous improvement. It is always easier for an ambitious professional committed to continuous improvement to work for an employer with a similar philosophy.

Summary:

This is an essential philosophy for an ambitious employee who wants to learn quickly and fast-track their progress with their current employer and in their future career.

33

Learn to negotiate and look for win/win outcomes

Traditionally, negotiating was regarded as some kind of black art that took place between employers and trade unions. However, negotiating is an aspect of business that happens at work every day, whether formally or informally. In the past, disagreements at work resulted in one individual or group winning and, consequently, another person or group losing.

When I started my career, nearly all of the Fortune 500 companies were managed by men, and most of these men were proponents of this win/lose model. Many of these male CEOs were lionised as role models of management. They addressed conferences and wrote books outlining the reasons for their successes. Thankfully, over time it was noticed that this formula was not sustainable and typically only led to short-term success, as evidenced by the fact that there was a continuous churn in the names of companies featuring in the Fortune 500 listings.

1. **Adopt best practice in negotiations and look for win-win outcomes.**

   Regardless of who you are negotiating with, try to move away from the traditional win/lose model and adopt the more sustainable win/win model. Companies are generally more consultative and participative nowadays, and this has given rise to a more collaborative rather than confrontational style of negotiation. Under this negotiation model, you are particularly attentive to the relationships involved in the negotiating process. You try to ensure that your relationship with the person you negotiate with is preserved. This provides a basis for an ongoing working relationship between both parties.

2. **Negotiate with your boss.**

   Although most of your interactions with your boss may seem like normal conversations, they often have an element of negotiation involved in them. You need to be able to identify when this element is present and be prepared to negotiate if you have an alternative point of view. Traditionally, new graduates would just do what they are told but many companies are now looking for more assertiveness in professional employees which involves being able to negotiate.

3. **Learn to negotiate with colleagues.**

   As per the previous point, this is often a case of realising when a discussion involves an element of negotiation, recognising your own requirements, and ensuring these are fully considered.

4. **Learn to say 'no.'**

   We covered this previously in the context of managing your time, and it is particularly relevant here. You have to learn this skill because if you do not, you will limit your effectiveness at work. You may develop a reputation for being very obliging, but if this involves you doing work that diverts you away from your key goals and objectives, then you will not be successful at work.

5. **Do research where necessary before you negotiate.**

If, for example, you wish to negotiate a salary increase, it will not be enough to request a salary increase just because you think you deserve it. You will need to justify your reasons for looking for an increase, especially if this is before the due date. This may involve external research establishing salary rates in your sector for people with your qualifications and experience. It may also involve clearly identifying what internal reasons you have to justify your request. This may mean identifying additional work you have successfully undertaken or some examples of exceptional performance that will support your case.

6. **Be assertive when you negotiate.**

There is no point in doing your research and preparing your case well if you do not present your arguments in a business-like and confident manner. Anything less will undermine your negotiating position. This applies equally to face-to-face negotiations and to written communications.

7. **Get trained in negotiation.**

It takes time to become an effective negotiator. You will need to get training in this area, and the sooner you get this training, the better. Again, your performance review is an ideal opportunity to request such training.

8. **Observe role models.**

Study good negotiators carefully. Try to adopt some of their negotiating techniques if some of these suit your operating style.

9. Keep your cool.

Regardless of how emotionally charged a negotiation process becomes, it is critical that you remain calm, especially if you encounter strong resistance and even personal animosity. If you lose your composure, you will weaken your negotiating position, and you could quickly damage your standing within the organisation.

Summary:

This is another of these core skills you will need to become competent in if you are to succeed in your first job and your career. The earlier you address this, the better. Adopt the present-day negotiating model, which tends to have more sustainable results than the traditional win/lose model.

34

Develop a sense of humour

All things being equal, most people prefer to deal with people they like, and people with a sense of humour often appear more likeable.

1. **Develop a sense of humour.**

   This point comes very naturally to many people, but this is not the case for some people. I realise that it is not easy to develop a sense of humour if you have started your working life without this particular quality. However, it could help you greatly if you could develop this quality even to a minor extent. As it happened, this was a quality that came easily to me over my career. It helped me to accept and come to terms with some of my many failings as a HR Manager and as a business owner.

2. **Do not take yourself too seriously and learn to laugh at yourself occasionally.**

   It is a great asset to be able to laugh at yourself, and having that quality will make your working life much more rewarding and enjoyable. It may not come naturally to you at the start of your working life, but you can learn to cultivate this important attribute as you settle into your first job. An ability to indulge in some gentle self-deprecation is seen as a likeable quality and is something you can learn with a little effort.

3. **Draw on your sense of humour, especially on bad days.**

   There will be many days at work over a forty-year career where everything seems to go against you and having a sense of humour may be the only redeeming factor you can cling to. There are days when Murphy's Law seems to apply, i.e. when anything that could go wrong does go wrong, and your ability to laugh at the absurdity of it all may be the only thing to keep you going through those tough days.

4. **People are drawn to people who have a sense of humour.**

   Like being friendly and approachable, a sense of humour means people are more inclined to help you out, give you the benefit of the doubt or give you a second chance. Hopefully, you will be able to experience how that can work in your favour if a little humour becomes part of your repertoire.

Summary:

Learning to develop a sense of humour and an ability not to take yourself too seriously will serve you well throughout your career. It is a quality that is particularly important to help get you through the bad days. It is one worth developing, even if it does not come naturally to you.

35

Provide excellent customer service

A. Internal Customer Service

1. **Provide excellent customer service internally as this is a prerequisite to providing it externally.**

   You need to look at your internal contacts as customers and treat them accordingly. Thankfully, the day is largely gone where companies only thought about the end customer and took much less interest in internal relationships.

2. **Treat your internal customers with respect, as this is one of the key requirements of your position.**

   It is increasingly recognised nowadays that a failure in that regard could adversely impact the wellbeing of the person you are dealing with. In turn, this could reduce the likelihood of them treating their internal and external customers professionally at all times.

3. **Treat your internal contacts well to indicate you are a team player.**

   You must continually show you are a team player. A failure in this regard could be regarded as showing a lack of respect for colleagues. It clearly shows a failure to recognise the interdependence of all roles within an organisation. Such a failure may result in you being let go or, at the very least, greatly inhibit your prospects within the company.

4. **Expect good customer service from fellow workers where you are their internal customer.**

This cuts both ways – if you provide good internal customer service, you are also entitled to expect it in return. If you do not receive this, you must address the issue before it gets out of hand. Ideally, if you experience a problem in this regard, you should address it in the first instance with the individual concerned. If this approach is unsuccessful, you should not let the situation persist. Address it with your manager and request their assistance in resolving it. You are only creating stress for yourself which is likely to worsen and come to a head later if it is not addressed. Parity of esteem is a prerequisite for a successful partnership relationship between customer and supplier.

Summary:
Most professional organisations now accept and implement the concept of the internal customer and recognise its relevance to the provision of excellent service to end customers. You need to align with this thinking which should be easy for you to adapt to as a new member of the workforce who is not burdened by old-fashioned views on this matter.

B. External Customer Service

1. **Understand you are an ambassador for your company when you deal directly with a customer.**

That is a very privileged position to be in but brings with it an additional level of responsibility. You need to be fully aware of this and keep it in mind at all times as your actions can have a bearing, not just on your own future, but on the future of all company employees.

2. **Always bring the right attitude to your dealings with customers.**

From my experience, this is not always the case. Some employees can sometimes see the customer as a problem rather than as the person who pays their wages. Employees and companies who display this kind of attitude are not going to get away with this approach, particularly nowadays, as customer demands and expectations continue to increase.

3. **Learn to 'go the extra mile' for customers.**

You need to develop this approach at all times, even where the customer is very demanding and has what may appear to you as unreasonable expectations. The old adage that 'the customer is always right' is not as dogmatically adhered to nowadays, but it still is a reasonable guideline to follow.

4. **Develop a partnership relationship with your customer with parity of esteem between supplier and customer.**

For this parity of esteem to become a reality, you should seek to become an expert in what you do and what you provide. Of course, this will take time to develop, but that should be your goal. Some recruitment consultants struggled with this parity of esteem concept in the recruitment industry, which I am familiar with. Unfortunately, some customers would look at all recruitment agencies in a negative light, which was unhelpful. However, if a consultant had self-esteem and a level of expertise, they would usually win over clients, including those customers who traditionally would have tarred all recruitment agencies with the same brush.

Summary:

Always go the extra mile and in doing so, seek to establish a parity or esteem in your relationship with all customers. If you are privileged enough to be in a customer-interfacing role, it is important to recognise yourself as being an ambassador for your employer and to commit yourself to providing an excellent level of service to your end customer. To ensure this, you must expect and demand the same from your internal customers.

36
Be patient (but not too patient!)

1. **Learn to be patient from the beginning of your working life.**

   One of my former colleagues retired recently after completing over forty years' service with their employer. As well as displaying great stamina, they also displayed great patience, which contributed significantly to their many achievements over the years.

2. **Recognise that great patience is required in the early stages of your first job.**

   This is a time when it is easy to become frustrated on realising how much you have to learn to become effective in your new job. You may also be frustrated by how slow the decision-making process can be, especially in larger organisations. As per the previous section, you will have to show more patience and assertiveness than you may have anticipated to get your ideas accepted.

3. **Accept if these necessary checks and balances do not suit your operating style.**

   If that is the case, after a couple of years you may decide to pursue your career in a smaller organisation where the decision-making process is quicker or is less complex.

4. **Understand that timing is everything.**

   Experienced professionals become very adept at reading the signals which indicate the time is right to propose a certain idea that they may have been considering for some time. Again, this is a skill that you must acquire as a new employee, and you can learn a lot by studying individuals with long service and a track record of getting things done.

5. **Understand that being patient and being a good team player often run together.**

Long-serving employees are naturally good at slowly garnering support for their ideas and knowing when to call on that support. Again, this ability to build alliances in promoting ideas is something you will have to develop and perfect over the years. If not, you will become frustrated as many of your good ideas may be passed over if you have not learned how to cultivate the necessary connections to get at least some of these ideas adopted.

6. **Be patient if you are trying to sell an idea to non-technical people or people with a different technical expertise.**

You need to take the time to look at your proposal from the point of view of someone who does not have expertise in your area but is an expert in what they do. Patient people are good at developing this broader perspective. As a result, they learn to present their ideas in a way that will be understood by those they are trying to persuade regardless of their particular area of expertise.

7. **Learn to be patient with yourself.**

Without this patience, you can easily become discouraged by the expertise of long-serving employees and the amount you have to learn. This may come as an unwelcome surprise and a setback to some newly-qualified professionals who may have assumed they would make rapid progress in the company from an early stage. You need to adjust to the reality that there is so much to learn and that your employer will want to see whether you can apply your academic knowledge in the real world of work. This may also test your patience with yourself as a new employee.

8. **Learn to be patient with your boss.**

You may be frustrated that your boss doesn't run with one of your ideas immediately, but you need to realise their responsibility will involve choosing between competing ideas for scarce resources within your department. Again, it is about putting yourself in your boss's shoes and seeing things from their point of view. If you learn to do this, it may encourage you to put more effort into presenting your ideas in a manner that may have broader appeal than the narrow perspective you may have adopted initially.

9. **Note my somewhat tongue-in-cheek advice of not to be too patient in the heading for this section.**

I have done so deliberately because I do not want new employees to lose sight of the important balance that has to be achieved between being patient while also getting things done. I have come across many people in positions of little or no accountability who seem to have a lot of patience but seem to achieve very little. I would not like to see any new employee fall into such a negative behaviour pattern early in their working life. You will not be retained in a demanding work environment if you do not get this balance right.

10. Recognise if you cannot develop the patience to succeed in a particular work environment.

In the horse racing world, there is an expression, 'horses for courses.' This recognises the reality that some horses do better on flat racecourses, whereas others prefer the greater test of stamina provided by a course with a stiff uphill finish. In my case, one of the reasons I started my own business is that I could see that I probably did not have the level of patience needed to continue my career beyond a certain point in a large corporate environment. If you feel that this applies to you at some stage in your career, you need to acknowledge this and look for a position in a more suitable company.

Summary:

Patience is one of the main qualities you will need to develop if you are to be successful throughout your career. In your working life, your patience will be tested on a daily basis, be it with yourself, your boss, your colleagues, or by policies, systems, and procedures. Studying one or two successful role models may help you to develop this very important quality.

37
Work effectively from home

1. **Adapt to working from home if your job calls for this.**
   This became the norm for many people since the onset of COVID-19 and some element of this is likely to continue as we enter into the endemic phase of the pandemic. The right to work from home, at least on a part time basis, is likely to be enshrined in legislation for many professions later this year. When this happens it will constitute a seismic change to the world of work as we understood it before the pandemic began. Although it is far from ideal for a recently qualified graduate, you need to adjust to it and implement the emerging best practice in working effectively from home.

2. **Co-operate with your employer and adapt to your working environment at home.**
   Initially, people were happy to pop a laptop on the kitchen table without taking lighting, seating, noise, and glare into consideration – in other words, the whole ergonomics of working from home. Your employer is now or soon will be considering the long-term situation in relation to employees working from home, and you must do the same.

3. **Avail of any remedial work that your employer is prepared to pay for.**
   Some progressive and highly profitable companies are offering to pay for some or all remedial work to ensure that their employees are working in a suitable home office envi-

ronment. You should avail of any such offers because they are in your best interest, as well as being of benefit to your employer. Even if your employer cannot afford these measures, you should try to ensure your work area is suitable for a prolonged period of working at home.

4. **Co-operate with your employer as they seek to address the insurance implications of working at home over an extended period.**

As a result of this, some companies are sending checklists to their employees to ensure that their company is implementing best practice in this area by ensuring that a part of your home is a suitable work environment.

5. **Ensure that the increasingly blurred lines between work and your personal life do not become even more blurred in a working from home scenario.**

Companies have a responsibility to ensure that employees have a life outside of work, but you must also be proactive in addressing this issue or your mental health could suffer. There is evidence that the always-on generation of employees is 'on' even more now. If you have concerns about this, raise them with your immediate boss so that you both have clarity as to when you will be online and when you will be unavailable. My recommendation would be that your boss would not contact you by phone or email outside of normal working hours, other than in very exceptional circumstances. If your employer doesn't suggest this, you should. It is likely that legislation will be enacted to address this issue after consultation with the relevant vested interest groups.

6. **Take positive steps to create a clear differentiation between your working life and your home life.**

For example, by putting your work items like your PC or files away at the end of the workday, you are less likely to be tempted to go back to them later on. You could also consider wearing work clothes while you are working and changing to civvies after that. I know some people find this helps to create a clear differentiation between their work life and personal life.

7. **Co-operate with efforts by your employer to keep employees informed and involved.**

Companies and employees are struggling to find a solution for the sense of isolation from colleagues that employees are feeling now that the initial novelty of working from home has worn off. Companies have to work harder at communicating with employees to ensure they still feel part of a team. Some are introducing fun events, as well as formal communications, to address this issue. Employees may have to take initiatives in this regard also. Connect with some of your colleagues online and look at ways of addressing this important issue.

8. **Pay particular attention to all aspects of your mental health.**

We addressed the importance of physical, mental, psychological and spiritual health issues earlier. You may have to be very proactive to ensure that you give even more attention to all of these if you are required to work from home on an ongoing basis.

Summary:

There are some major advantages of working from home. The pandemic gave many people a chance to look at their work-life balance, especially those who used to have very long commutes. However, some potentially serious downsides are emerging in the area of mental health. Even if your company is not proactive in addressing this issue, you must take the initiative in addressing your needs in this area before it becomes a problem for you. In particular, you must be proactive in taking steps to create some clear boundaries between your work life and your personal life.

38
Beware of multitasking

The ability to multitask has been seen as a desirable attribute for an employee until recently. However, the issue is more complex than simply being regarded as a good or a bad thing.

1. **Be able to juggle several issues at the same time.**
   Because of the complex nature of organisations, it is necessary in most roles to be able to carry a demanding and varied workload. As covered in a previous section, companies need employees who have the flexibility and agility in their approach to be able to readily adapt to the changing needs of their role and the organisation.

2. **Multitasking works best in matters of routine.**
   If a job has very clear practices and procedures such as may be outlined on a checklist, multitasking across similar tasks is not only viable, but it is also desirable. As a newly employed professional, you may be assigned these kind of tasks until you are ready to undertake more complex tasks. You should be able to show the necessary flexibility and adaptability to perform such routine tasks.

3. **Don't multitask if you are involved in problem-solving.**
   Complex problems require considering a wide range of possible solutions, and each of these potential solutions will require considerable analysis. They may also require consultations with your own manager, departmental colleagues, or colleagues in other departments. The point is, there are a limited number of such projects that anyone can work

on at a time, especially if the problems are to be given the detailed consideration they warrant. In the case of a major project, that project may be your sole focus because of the complexity involved.

4. **Don't multitask in complex decision-making situations.**

Again, routine decisions should not be an issue for you, but you must recognise where a matter you are working on is complex and where a quick decision may be inappropriate. You may need to take time to weigh up different options, reflect on the matter, and consult with colleagues extensively before arriving at a decision.

For example, when making decisions in HR in terms of hiring a senior executive, complex matters which required detailed consideration and consultation before a decision could be made include the interviewing process, the consultation process, the comparison of excellent candidates and the assessment of the 'fit' with the company culture and values. 'Recruit in haste and repent at your leisure' is a saying that highlights the hazards of making a quick recruitment decision. This can be applied to complex decision-making in all departments of a company.

5. **Remember, effectiveness comes before efficiency.**

As we covered in the time management section, as a professional, you are primarily employed to deal effectively with the important issues more than efficiently dealing with less significant problems. Multitasking is not working for you if you fail to fully address the important issues.

6. Quality takes precedence over quantity.

As a professional, you are expected to get things right the first time. You need to be wary of multitasking as it could affect the quality of your work. If you become aware that this risk is present, you need to discuss it with your boss before a problem arises and request a reduction in the number of projects you are working on.

Summary:

Flexibility, adaptability, and agility are all essential qualities for you to display in your new role. However, be careful in your anxiety to present yourself in a positive light, that you do not multitask in a situation where the quality of your work could be compromised.

39

Be persistent

1. **Make a conscious effort to develop persistence.**

   This is essential for you to be successful in your first job. It is also essential if you want to realise your potential in your working life.

2. **Display persistence in your dealings with colleagues.**

   Persistence is becoming increasingly important as interdependence grows both in business and in life in general. For you, this will increasingly mean trying to achieve results with the cooperation of other people as very few roles nowadays are single contributor roles which have limited interaction with other employees. This is particularly the case as you enter the management ranks.

3. **Be persistent in dealing with bureaucracy at work.**

   Achieving results in an increasingly bureaucratic world requires a high level of persistence in situations where you may sometimes feel like throwing in the towel. One of the reasons I started my own business after thirteen years in multinational companies was because of the time it often took to get things done due to the extent of the bureaucracy in long-established companies. Much of this is very necessary, but it does call for great persistence, tenacity, and patience to 'work the system' if you are the kind of person who wants to bring about significant changes in a large employer.

4. **Be persistence in understanding the perspective of a person who disagrees with your proposed course of action.**

Organisations, and particularly large organisations, are complex entities that are set up in such a way to ensure that there are adequate checks and balances in place to ensure they are run to the highest professional standards. Unfortunately, when you are trying to get something done in a hurry, you may find it hard to appreciate the responsibilities of someone who wants to ensure that you are not taking any shortcuts.

5. **Be persistent if you wish to persuade your manager to look for approval to buy an expensive piece of equipment.**

The number of forms you will have to complete, meetings you will have to attend, presentations you will have to make, setbacks you will have to encounter, may all cause you to wonder whether it is worth all of the effort involved. However, if you are determined to be successful, you will need to understand that this is all part of the process of getting things done in large and very complex organisations.

6. **Be persistent in applying for promotional opportunities.**

This is particularly important where you may have been passed over several times. Although being unsuccessful is always a setback, you should look for feedback any time this happens so that you can fine-tune your interview performance for the future. Every ambitious professional has setbacks, but it is how each person handles these setbacks and, specifically, the persistence they display in overcoming setbacks which will often decide which person advances in their career and which person simply gives up applying for promotional opportunities.

7. **Interpret a rejection as meaning 'Not Now' rather than 'Never.'**

   This is necessary because timing is often the reason an idea is rejected. The same idea, something very similar or something presented differently, can often be successful at a later date.

8. **Be persistent when part of a project team when there is agreement about the end goal but not about the process.**

   Being persistent may ensure the team embarks on the right track rather than wasting a lot of time in an unproductive manner. Even if the consensus is that your approach is wrong, you should continue to argue for it, but in doing so, try to present your ideas more persuasively than you did in the first instance.

9. **Be persistent in the face of multiple setbacks and rejections.**

   If you strongly believe in the proposal you are advocating, you must not relent, even if it feels like an uphill struggle. You need to trust your gut instinct in these situations, dig deep and regard this as a character-building opportunity rather than a reason for giving up.

Summary:

Persistence is one of the most essential qualities you will require if you are to enjoy a long and successful career. I suggest you start developing this quality from day one as it is one of the most visible ways you can differentiate yourself from other people who wish to progress their careers within the organisation. Persistence is particularly important when you have to overcome several significant setbacks, which may cause a less persistent person to give up.

40

Be assertive

1. **Resolve to always be assertive at work.**
   One of the first things you are likely to discover early in your first job is that having a good idea will often not be enough to get it implemented. You will quickly learn that the idea will have to be presented in an assertive and persuasive manner.

2. **Align assertiveness with persistence, and you are more likely to be successful.**
   The combination of these two attributes is very powerful and will greatly increase your effectiveness as a communicator.

3. **Be particularly assertive and persistent if you work in a hierarchical company where it is harder to be heard.**
   Being very assertive may be essential to be heard in that kind of work environment. Not everyone has that level of assertiveness or wants to be that persistent, hence the importance of knowing about the company culture before accepting a position in such a company.

4. **Be assertive in your written communications.**
   This is especially important in very large organisations where you may not have direct access to a decisionmaker and where you are required to communicate your idea in writing. As well as having a well-researched and thought-through case, you need to communicate this in an asser-

tive and persuasive manner. Use action verbs in the present tense and avoid 'weasel words' such as hopefully, possibly, maybe, sometimes, etc., as these kinds of words suggest you have little or no conviction in your idea.

5. **Ensure your call-to-action is crystal clear in all forms of communication or it will be passed over.**

    As a new graduate, you may need to look for guidance in this area from your boss or a more experienced colleague to ensure you provide the necessary clarity for your proposal to be fully considered.

6. **Provide a clear cost/benefit analysis for any actions you are advocating.**

    In particular, if you can convince people of an early return on a proposed investment, you will have a much better chance of getting your proposal approved, assuming you have presented it assertively and persuasively.

7. **Be succinct and to the point, anticipate objections and be ready to respond to them decisively and convincingly.**

    Many a good idea never got off the ground because easily anticipated questions were not considered or replied to in an unassertive manner. This clearly highlighted the absence of proper preparation in either the content or style of communication.

8. **Be very clear where assertiveness ends and aggression takes over.**

    Regardless of how strongly you feel about an idea and how frustrated you are by the rejection of or ambivalence to your idea, you must not become aggressive. If you do become aggressive, your idea will be overlooked, but your aggression will be noticed. If this pattern of behaviour were to be repeated, questions might well arise regarding your suitability as a long-term employee.

9. **Remain assertive and avoid becoming aggressive if you get into a conflict situation with another employee.**

By all means, be as assertive as you need to be, but if you can see that open conflict is in danger of arising, you need to take yourself out of the situation and take some time to consider what to do next. You may decide to approach the individual again when and if they have cooled off, or you may need to refer the matter to your boss or HR.

Summary:
Being assertive is a core skill of an effective employee, and you should decide to start acquiring that skill from day one. Look out for role models who are particularly good at getting their ideas accepted, be that verbally or in writing. Study them closely and try to understand their modus operandi, and adopt the points that will fit in with your personality and communication style. Never cross the dividing line between assertiveness and aggression.

41

Be yourself

In the course of this book, I have outlined a series of dos and don'ts about how you should conduct yourself at work. I believe each of these points has merit, but I firmly believe that this particular point is the most important.

1. **Be your own unique self.**

   No one in this world has the exact same combination of skills, personal qualities, and attitudes that you have. It is vitally important that you honour and respect your uniqueness by putting your own personal stamp on your work.

2. **Build on your unique strengths.**

   These strengths have served you well in your life to date, and they are something to build on in your new world of work. These strengths were the reason you were recruited by your employer, and because of this, your employer will want you to develop these strengths and apply them in the work environment. While some employers look for a greater degree of conformity than others, none seek to subjugate employees' individuality to the point where they are trying to create clones.

3. **Learn from others but do not attempt to imitate anyone else.**

   As mentioned many times throughout this book, there is much to be learned from others in terms of developing particular skills and qualities, but that is very different from actually trying to imitate someone else. A colleague or a boss has their own unique combination of strengths that work for them. For you to uncritically adopt these qualities and subjugate your own unique qualities in the process would be a serious mistake, and it would also do you a great disservice.

4. Don't imitate others as it is unsustainable.

Even if you were to attempt to imitate a very successful work colleague, this would be unsustainable because, in addition to having your own unique strengths, you have your own unique values and beliefs, which must be honoured and respected. Imitation is not the way to do this.

5. Use this book selectively.

There is much that is generic in this book, but several points reflect my unique experience and my particular values and beliefs. Take what you consider useful from the generic material and adapt it to suit your unique qualities, skills, attitudes, values, and beliefs.

Summary:

While it is a good idea to learn from others, it is fundamentally wrong to try to imitate them and to subjugate your own unique self in the process. Be your own unique self and be proud to be so.

42
Become a go-to professional

1. **Resolve to become a go-to professional.**

   This is not going to apply to all employees, but I would recommend it to someone with a particularly strong work ethic. I see it as something that you should set out to achieve as such a person is invaluable in any department because of their demeanour, flexibility, and expertise.

2. **Accept that it will take time to become recognised in this way.**

   Be patient and assiduous as you slowly but steadily build up your knowledge and skillset. You are a graduate with much to learn, but if you apply yourself diligently, you will gradually build up a body of knowledge that will lead to you being seen as an expert in your field.

3. **Set out to be an employee who not only meets their objectives but often exceeds them as well.**

   This may not suit everyone as many people will be satisfied to achieve their objectives, but go-to experts always go further, and that is what makes them experts. In addition, while you may aspire to be an expert in the earlier stage of your career, your values may change over time, and basic competence may then become your standard.

4. **Develop a mentality of 'going the extra mile.'**

   If you wish to attain go-to status, you must ensure that you always do everything within your power to exceed at every task you are assigned. This is a big ask that will not suit a lot of people because of the extra effort that it requires.

5. **Acquire this reputation within your department and in your interaction with other departments.**

   This will make you stand out as a rising star within the organisation and position you well for internal promotion. It is important because it is usually the experts within a department that are successful in internal interviews for promotional opportunities.

6. **Understand that the opportunity to stand out and make a greater impact increases at a senior level in the company.**

   Should you retain the ambition to be a go-to expert as you progress up the managerial ranks, your potential to really make a difference will increase, as will the demands on you and the risk that your work will begin to intrude on your personal life. Because of this, it is something you have to continually keep under review to ensure you are happy with your work-life balance. If you allow work to intrude too much into your personal life, this will eventually have an impact on your working life, making you stale and reducing your effectiveness at work.

7. **Seek out further training and education on an ongoing basis.**

   You will have to be prepared to proactively look for internal and external training and further education to stand out in your department to acquire the go-to moniker. If you do not, someone else will.

8. **Consider changes in your personal circumstances when deciding how far you want to progress within the company and your career.**

You are operating in a dynamic situation where things are changing in your company, your career, and your personal life. This means that you will need to continually review how these changes are impacting your life. If you are not comfortable with some of these changes, and they are causing you stress, you may need to make adjustments that will bring greater equilibrium to your life. These could be changes you need to make at work, at home, or a combination of both.

Summary:

It is good for you as a new employee to set out to be an expert in what you do. This will open up other opportunities for you within the company. It is up to you to decide how far you wish to progress within the company and your career, and what price you are willing to pay to progress as you desire. This is something you will need to keep under careful review as your personal circumstances change.

43

Adopt a business development approach

1. **Adopt a broader business development perspective of your role, particularly if it involves customer interaction.**

   Taking a macro view of your role, rather than a narrow micro view, is in your best interest with your current employer and with future employers as well. Increasingly, more and more companies see all professional employees who have any contact with customers as potential business developers.

2. **Note a passing comment from a client, as it may indicate a plan for the client to expand its operations.**

   This may point to a business development opportunity that you can relay to your colleagues in sales who will welcome the 'heads up' even if they are already aware of the customer's plans.

3. **Note where a customer mentions a downturn in their business.**

   This may have a negative effect on your employer's business, but it could also point to a potential business development opportunity. For example, in my former company's recruitment and HR services business, a downturn in a client's business often led to an opportunity in the HR side of my company's business.

4. **This business development perspective should come more easily to you if you are a natural companywide team player.**

   This will be even more likely if a whole team approach is an integral part of the company culture and is reflected in its company values.

5. **View meetings with clients as a way of ascertaining emerging trends in the market.**

   This could give your company an important insight into an emerging business opportunity at an embryonic stage and may persuade your company to develop a new product offering before your competitors.

6. **Use this approach to identify process improvement opportunities that may benefit your internal customers.**

   Sometimes an improvement in the design of a product can result in it being easier or cheaper to manufacture, which could lead to improvements in productivity and profitability.

7. **Accept the opportunity to work in cross-functional teams if it is offered to you.**

   This will also give you the chance to develop that 'bigger picture' orientation that more and more companies are looking for. It should give you a better understanding of the business and help you to better understand the relevance of your present job. It may also point to a potential new direction for your career with your present employer or with another employer in the future.

8. **Develop this thought process to better understand the workings of the business.**

   Employees who have that orientation can naturally apply it in any work environment that encourages a 'big picture' orientation. This approach can be seen very clearly in employees who were raised in a family business where everyone is expected to contribute.

9. **Develop this kind of thought process so that you are more likely to identify a business opening at a later stage in your career.**

   This often happens and can lead to a whole new career and the satisfaction of running your own business. It may seem a long way away from you now, as you start your first job, but many business owners started as you are now and never thought they would someday start their own business. That was the case with me. My experience in HR gave me an insight into a potential opening for a recruitment and HR services company providing a service to multinational companies in the west of Ireland initially and nationally at a later stage.

Summary:

Although this may not seem an obvious point, if your job does not involve dealing with the end customer, you will at least have dealings with internal customers. Please try to adopt this business development attitude because it is something that will stand to you throughout your working life. If you have adopted a team-player approach, this kind of thought process should come naturally to you. Fostering this business development perspective could help you identify a promising business development opportunity for yourself at some stage in your working life.

44

Find a mentor and a coach

A. Find A Mentor

1. **Find a mentor who will take you under their wing and guide you in your first job.**

   Ideally and usually, your mentor is your manager, but that is not always the case.

2. **Be proactive and draw on the benefit of that person's considerable experience and wisdom.**

   It is important that you are attentive to the advice and direction of your mentor. Your mentor is usually highly experienced, and there is much to be learned from such a seasoned professional.

3. **Run your ideas past your mentor, especially at the start of your career.**

   In doing so, you often receive invaluable guidance that ensures you do not have to go through the painful process of trial and error that was often the norm in the past.

4. **Listen to your mentor, who can steer you through the complex labyrinth of dos and don'ts that exist in every organisation.**

   As a new employee, you will not initially be aware of many of these dos and don'ts. You could easily and inadvertently fall foul of some of these without the guidance of a clued-in mentor.

Summary:

Find a good mentor and learn from them. They have a wealth of experience and knowledge and will usually be willing to allow you to tap into that expertise.

B. Find A Business Coach

1. **Consider whether you need a business coach.**

    A business coach is a professionally qualified practitioner who typically works outside the company in their own business or as one of a team of coaches. Usually, as a new professional, you will not need a coach, and your manager or mentor should provide you with sufficient guidance at an early stage in your career. However, if your manager is not interested in mentoring and you do not have access to another mentor, you could request that you be given access to a coach.

    Identifying a suitable coach and developing a good rapport with them could provide a huge boost to your career at a very formative stage. Guidance from such a person could help your route to promotion because you have access to a role model who, as the saying goes, 'has been there and done that.'

2. **Speak to your boss if the off-the-shelf company training programmes do not meet your training needs.**

    Again, this should not be necessary during the initial stages of your career as most major companies have a wide range of high-quality trainers and training programmes. However, if this is not the case or you wish to progress your career more quickly, you could request access to a personal coach. An effective coach can provide a customised service that a typical training programme cannot address as each trainee on a training programme has very different training needs.

3. **Attend any customised training programmes that your employer provides.**

These are usually better than off-the-shelf training programmes as they are more customised to address the needs of the attendees.

4. **Avail of a dedicated coach who can give guidance to help you to fast-track your professional development.**

Even if your employer doesn't provide this kind of pro bono coaching experience, you should seriously consider identifying a suitable coach and pay for the service yourself. A good coach will enter into a challenging contractual relationship with the professional, which should help to fast-track their professional development. A coach will bring a broad industry perspective to their role, which will benefit you more than just getting a concentrated in-company perspective. Better still, they may have experience across several business sectors, and they may even have some overseas experience as well.

Summary:

Having a business coach, as opposed to a life coach, is an important part of your professional development and can help to fast-track your career progression. As a general rule, I would highly recommend it over off-the-shelf training programmes, especially after you have attended some customised training programmes and acquired several years of work experience.

45

Be compassionate

Your working life, like all other aspects of your life, may be tough at times and sometimes you need to accept this rather than continually rail against it by pointing out its unfairness. This is why I have included this topic, although it is not one usually found in books about work. However, I do believe it is a subject that will get more attention in the future as the importance of one's overall wellbeing becomes more generally recognised and accepted.

1. **Develop self-compassion.**

   If you have perfectionist tendencies, as I did, you may find it hard to accept when you make mistakes or when you overlook something you were supposed to do. It is right that you should regret such mistakes or oversights and seek to take corrective action to reduce the chances of such issues arising in the future. However, there is absolutely no point in beating yourself up over such matters, and a little self-compassion would be much more appropriate. You are a human being, and as such, you will make mistakes.

2. **Learn to forgive yourself.**

   Rather than berating yourself over what sometimes may be a relatively minor matter, you need to learn to forgive yourself. I know this may not come easily to you with your track record of achievement, but you need to develop this quality. Otherwise, you may be at risk of exaggerating your failings and not giving yourself adequate recognition for your many achievements.

3. **Being able to admit to mistakes and to accept weakness is actually a strength.**

This may not seem obvious to you in the beginning, but it is both a strength and a sign of maturity when you can do this. It is also a sign of recognition and acceptance of your humanity. I feel slightly hypocritical raising this point as it is one I often struggled with. For some reason, I was quite good at accepting other people's failings but not very good at accepting my own. This inability to accept some of my weaknesses was stressful for me at times, and I do not want to see you make the same mistake.

4. **Have compassion for yourself if you are having a bad day.**

While it is right that you should expect high standards of yourself and try to be energetic and enthusiastic at all times, life just doesn't always work out like that. You are a human being, not a robot. While you should rightly aspire to give your best every day, your best may sometimes be diminished by health issues, personal problems, difficulties with colleagues, or with your boss. Accepting this and doing your best in the throes of these types of issues is part of life. Obviously, if a problem that is causing you to be below par continues to be an issue, you may have to take corrective action, but if it is only a short-term issue, some self-compassion is needed.

5. **Learn to show compassion to others.**

It would not be appropriate if you could only show compassion to yourself and not show the same level of compassion to your boss or your work colleagues. They, too, are human (yes, even bosses!!) and will have days when they are not at their best for various reasons. You need to be able to recognise when this is the case and factor that into your dealings with them. Unless you are a very intuitive person, you may not always pick up on these things, but with experience and a bit of empathy, you should recognise the signals most of the time and cut them some slack in the short term. As in your own case, corrective action may be needed, especially if the person concerned fails to address their issues after some time, but that is usually a matter for them, their boss, or HR.

Summary:

Having some compassion for yourself and your work colleagues is important. Throughout your working life, you will encounter occasions where you or your colleagues are not performing to their usual standards. You will need acceptance, maturity and compassion to navigate your way through these kinds of situations.

46

Continue formal education and join a professional body

A. Continue Formal Education

1. **Resume your formal education if you want to progress your career.**

   This is probably not something you want to consider at this stage, having just completed your degree, but even if you decide to take a year or two off from your studies, I think you need to address it at that stage. The longer you postpone the decision to continue your formal education, the harder it will be to do so, and the less time you may also have for your professional advancement. The danger of not undertaking further education is that your hard-earned knowledge can quickly become redundant. You must take steps to keep up to date with the latest research and findings in your area of expertise as new knowledge is constantly being discovered in every profession.

2. **Avail of any financial incentives your employer may offer to encourage you to resume your studies.**

   This can make it more feasible for you to stay current with new developments in your field and removes a valid reason that some people may have for not staying up to date in their field of expertise.

3. Continue your professional development to make a positive statement of intent.

By doing this, you are clearly indicating your wish to stay current in your field, and you are also highlighting your ambition to progress within the company. This is important because if internal promotions arise within your company, those employees who have undertaken or are undertaking further third-level education are more likely to be successful in the internal interview process.

Summary:
I recommend you make the decision to resume your formal education within a year or two of completing your initial degree. This will make you stand out as someone professional and determined to stay at the top of your profession.

B. Join A Professional Body

1. Join or maintain membership in the professional body most relevant to your profession.

Again this is an association that can be of benefit to you throughout your career. Most companies will cover the membership fees of their professional employees, which can make it more feasible and more attractive to join or maintain your membership. By being part of a professional body, you will be on their mailing list for any professional publications they produce, which will help keep your professional knowledge up to date.

Many professional bodies have excellent monthly, bimonth-ly, or quarterly publications which contain thought-pro-voking articles based on the latest research in their particular field.

2. **Adopt the code of ethics of your professional body.**

This should inform and guide your professional behaviour throughout your career.

I was a member of the CIPD for all of my career, and I found it to be a great source of professional support and insight into best practices in my field.

3. **Attend seminars and conferences organised by your professional body.**

As well as keeping you current on the latest developments in your field, these events are important opportunities to maintain and develop your professional network.

Summary:

Being part of a professional body should be obligatory for any professional. It provides you with a code of practice, access to seminars and conferences, and excellent networking opportunities with fellow professionals.

47

Manage your ego

1. **Develop your self-esteem but do not develop an ego.**

   Although this is an important point, in my experience, it isn't usually as relevant to new employees as it can be for more seasoned professionals and particularly managers. You will need considerable self-esteem and self-worth to cope with the challenges of a typical working day, but one thing you will not need is a big ego, as this could adversely affect your dealings with your work colleagues.

2. **Do not compare yourself to world leaders with king-size egos and reassure yourself that you are nothing like that.**

   Of course, you may not be like that as you start your career, but it is important to remember that many of these leaders didn't start out that way either. Their egos gradually expanded, often on the back of some initial success.

3. **Be wary of following successful business leaders with big egos who are put forward as role models.**

   In the past, many aspiring professionals were encouraged to emulate such role models, but I would caution you against being overly impressed by such people as they are often not team players. It is interesting to note that many of the celebrated business leaders, who would have featured on the cover of Fortune 500 in the 1970s and 1980s, were dismissed or encouraged to move on later in their careers because their personal qualities and characteristics were not sustainable in the longer term. The rate of change in society and business has dramatically increased in recent years. It is likely to continue to do so, and this is having a major influence on the profile of successful business leaders emerging of late.

4. **Don't become known as a person who claims undue credit for success and distances themselves from any blame.**

   This type of behaviour is often exhibited by managers and professionals with big egos. You will quickly lose the respect of your team if you resort to such tactics, and in extreme cases, you may even lose your job.

5. **Avoid adopting executives in companies with autocratic cultures as role models.**

   You may even make good progress emulating someone like this in such a company in the short term, but after a while, you may find yourself not making any more progress. You may begin to realise that people may not want to work with you because of your egocentric approach. The number of companies with this kind of work culture is dwindling rapidly, so executives in these types of companies are not recommended as role models.

6. **Be aware that some initial success can change some people and cause them to stop using the very qualities that contributed to this success.**

   Human nature being what it is, some people allow success 'to go to their head.' If you have some initial success, you will need to be on your guard not to make this understandable and very common mistake.

7. Surround yourself with people who will alert you if your ego is expanding.

Throughout your career, it will be an advantage to you if you surround yourselves with people inside and outside of work who will help to keep your feet firmly on the ground. Such people will usually 'mark your card' if they see too much ego emerging in you, and you should take their counsel on board. On the subject of ego, I would like to draw your attention to a good piece of advice I heard many years ago which is relevant to a person rising through the ranks in an organisation – 'Be nice to people on the way up because you may meet them on the way down!'

Summary:

Although ego is still extolled in leaders in political and business life, this is something that is changing and will continue to change. I believe it is ultimately bad for society and businesses to view these kinds of leaders as role models. So I am cautioning you at an early stage of your career to be grounded in yourself and to select role models who are modest, genuinely humble, inclusive in their management style, and who are able to take success in their stride.

48

Become a competent interviewee

1. **Become competent as an interviewee as you are likely to do several internal and external interviews throughout your career.**

   People not only change jobs much more frequently nowadays, but they also change their careers more often. This means that you are likely to be in the role of interviewee many times. If you are to be successful in this regard, you will have no alternative but to develop competence in this area. You may think you do not need to address this as you have landed your first job in the face of much competition. That is understandable as you clearly must have some expertise as an interviewee. However, to progress to more senior roles within your company or in another company, you will need more expertise as an interviewee than would be expected of a graduate applying for their first position.

2. **Apply most of Section 28 on presentation skills to attain competence as an interviewee.**

   Review that section in detail and pick out the key pointers which apply to interviews. I think you may find they all apply because there is a definite trend to include a short presentation segment in interviews, especially at a senior level. This usually involves the applicant making a short presentation at the start of the interview, which then forms the basis for many of the questions at the interview.

3. Thorough preparation is essential before attending any interview.

This is easier for internal interviews as you will know a lot about the company and a certain amount about the job. However, there is a danger that this insider knowledge could lead to a level of complacency which may result in you failing to prepare thoroughly for the interview. You need to learn everything you can about the job. You must be fully prepared for any questions that may arise at the interview. If the interview is for a job where an incumbent is moving to a new role internally or externally, you need to learn everything you can from them about the role. You need to find out why they are moving to a new role, especially if the move is an external role.

Even if they are moving internally, you will want to know why, especially if they weren't in the position for long. You need to realise that you may not always get the full story behind a move for a variety of reasons. You need to trust your gut instinct if you feel there may have been a personality clash with the boss, which caused the incumbent to look for a new position. If the incumbent is moving to a lateral position, you should check out their reasoning more thoroughly. It may be they want a broader understanding of the business, but it may be they just weren't happy in that role or with that boss.

If the position you are applying for is an external one, then you will have to do lots of research on both the company and the role before attending the interview. That said, and as previously advised, I wouldn't generally recommend looking for such a role within two years of starting your first job as a newly-qualified professional unless you have a compelling reason for doing so.

4. Maintain good eye contact at interviews.

Maintaining eye contact suggests you have confidence in yourself and in what you are saying. It also communicates to the interviewer(s) that you are comfortable in your own skin, and you probably have good interpersonal skills. It also suggests you are being truthful as it is hard for interviewees to maintain eye contact if they are not honest when answering a question.

5. NEVER say anything negative about a previous employer.

If you speak negatively about a previous employer, this will set off alarm bells in most interviewers as they will obviously wonder how you will speak of them in the future. It also gives rise to questions about your judgment that you would freely offer such information about a company that you accepted a position with at one stage and which you may have been with for several years.

This is an absolute no-no. Please do not make this frequently-made mistake. Even if the interviewer is very searching in their questions, you need to be discreet in your replies, especially if you were with the company for some time.

6. Follow up.

If you apply for a job internally or externally, it can sometimes help to follow up to confirm your interest in the role. For example, if you interview externally through a recruitment agency, ring the consultant you are dealing with and ask them to advise the client that you were happy with the interview, that you are still interested, and may even have an increased level of interest in the position.

7. If your application is unsuccessful, find out why.

This is a very important point as you may get valuable feedback that may help you at future interviews. It should be very easy to get this feedback where you are applying for an internal role. For external roles, you may have to be persistent as some employers do not wish to elaborate on their reasons for not selecting someone, but many still do, and their feedback could be very helpful to you.

As a former HR Manager and the former owner of a recruitment consultancy, I was always impressed by people who followed up in this manner. In the latter capacity, I came across many cases where companies went back to a candidate at a later date who had respectfully followed up looking for feedback on their initial, unsuccessful interview.

Summary:
This is another skill that you need to achieve competence in if you are to secure the position you are interested in as you put together the building blocks of a successful career. Review Section 28 on presentation skills as most of the points covered there also apply in relation to improving your skills as an interviewee.

49

Avoid groupthink

This is a problem in some organisations, and when carried to extremes, it has led to the demise of many organisations which had been successful over a long period of time. This success sometimes led to hubris, complacency or an uncritical acceptance of the corporate view. This often led to companies not seeing the problems this was causing until it was too late, and the company could not be saved.

1. **Avoid succumbing to a groupthink culture.**

   I realise how difficult this is for a rookie as you will naturally want to go along with the consensus, especially as you have so little experience. You will understandably be inclined to go along with the views of more experienced colleagues. I hope that as you gain more experience, you will trust your gut and speak up if you believe the consensus view is wrong.

2. **Argue your case. Stick to your guns.**

   It is difficult to argue against consensus views, if you do so, it is particularly important to present your arguments clearly and logically. Sometimes these points will be accepted by your manager or your colleagues, but if not and you still believe your view is correct, you may need more supporting evidence, or you may need to present your arguments in a more convincing manner.

3. **Avoid being seen as a crank.**

   While independent thinking is usually encouraged in most well-run organisations, you should not carry it to extremes where you are in regular disagreement with the company, your boss or colleagues.

4. **Pick your battles carefully.**

   Some issues are clearly more important than others. Focus only on the key issues and let other, less important issues pass. If you become seen as someone who has the courage to proffer an opposing viewpoint in a convincing manner on an important matter, you will gain respect in most well-run businesses. However, if you continually take an opposing view, your credibility will suffer, and your suitability as an employee will come into question.

5. **Consider your future in a company with a strong group-think culture.**

   Groupthink is another indicator of weak management. If it is embedded in your company, you need to seriously consider whether you have a long-term future in such an organisation. You may be better joining a new and more vibrant company where your independent thinking is valued rather than looked upon with suspicion. In addition, companies with a strong groupthink culture are at risk of not seeing the need for change before it is too late for them to do so. You do not want your career to be adversely affected by such an outcome.

6. **Look for a change of department if groupthink is confined to your department.**

It sometimes happens that this is the case. Certain functions may tend to generate this type of culture. Sometimes managers prefer this operating style and may not be encouraged to change it if the department is performing effectively. If this is the case, and you do not feel you can grow in that environment, applying for a transfer to another department which seems to have a more open style of management may be an option to consider, rather than deciding to leave the organisation.

Summary:

It is important that you are part of an organisation that allows for independent thinking. This kind of thinking is needed to bring about timely changes in products, processes, policies, and procedures. It is good practice to be continually alert to the dangers of groupthink in any department or any company.

50
Leave on good terms

Although I have highlighted some of the benefits of having a long career with one employer, the reality is that most people change jobs a number of times in their career. In fact, nowadays, new graduates are likely to not only change jobs many times, but they are more likely to change careers at least once in their working life. That said, changing jobs is not a decision to be taken lightly. You need to be sure that leaving is the best option open to you before you decide to hand in your notice. You should consider looking for a job in another department if you have an issue with your boss. However, if the company's culture is not a good fit for you or you feel you have learned what you can and would benefit from a fresh challenge, then you are probably right to leave. Should you decide to leave and get a new job offer, I want to give you some very important advice that some employees do not always follow when they decide to leave their employer.

1. **Leave your employer on good terms.**

   In their excitement of securing a new and potentially more fulfilling role, many employees try to leave their employer in a hurry by not giving the agreed period of notice as specified in their employment contract. While it is understandable that you may be keen to start your new job as soon as possible, it is totally unacceptable and unprofessional to leave your employer without serving your notice period unless your employer freely agree to this. If I was your new employer and you proposed to break your contract of employment with your existing employer, I would not allow you to do this. I would also have concerns that you would even suggest as much.

2. **Do not be pressurised into starting your new job within your notice period.**

While it is understandable that your new employer would want you to start with them as soon as possible, it is a poor reflection on them if they encourage you to leave your employer within the agreed notice period. Equally so, you should not give in to pressure to leave early from a recruitment agency acting on behalf of your new employer.

3. **Be as flexible as possible during your notice period.**

If your employer wants you to train in a replacement, put in the effort to impart as much information as possible to that person. Try to tidy up any loose ends so that your employer is not left in the lurch in relation to any aspect of your role.

4. **Work conscientiously during your notice period.**

Although your thoughts may understandably drift towards your new job, it is important that you work diligently during your notice period. Some people make the mistake of reducing their commitment during this time. I would caution against this. It is disrespectful to your employer, to your boss, and to your colleagues. It is also disrespectful to yourself and reflects poorly on your work ethic.

5. **Remember you may need a reference from your first employer at a later date.**

Many employees forget that at some stage, a prospective employer may want to check references with previous employers. In that scenario, how you left a company may be remembered many years later and may colour the reference that is given. As well as being professional about how you leave, you need to see the bigger picture and understand how a hasty exit or a less than committed effort in your notice period could work against you. As a previous HR Manager, I saw this happen in a couple of situations. Also in my time running a recruitment and HR consultancy, I often took references that were less positive than they might have been had a person worked diligently through their required notice period.

Your employer hired you and gave you a good job that meant a lot to you over many years. They also trained you, paid you well, and honoured their side of the contract of employment. You should do the same.

Summary:

Do not make this fairly regular mistake of not giving the required notice period or reducing your commitment during your notice period. If you do this, it will reflect poorly on you, and it could have adverse consequences for you many years later.

Part Two

Miscellaneous topics and suggestions

In this part of the book, I wish to address 20 miscellaneous topics which can arise at work. You will need to be ready to deal with these topics as effectively as I hope you will deal with the 50 pointers I have already outlined.

1
Office politics

There are politics at play in all organisations. This is the case even in those organisations where the management works hard to avoid office politics getting a significant foothold in the company.

My advice to you is to be diplomatic at all times but to steer clear of people who try to get you to take sides with one individual against another or with one group of employees against another. You are being paid to do a job, do that job, and politely decline to get involved in anything that may distract you from doing your job.

I am fully aware of how unintentionally a person can be lured into the dangerous world of office politics. Such situations could have adverse consequences resulting in a person being seen as a troublemaker when that was never their intention.

Many organisations, particularly those with a weak management team and/or limited accountability, are rife with office politics which can become entrenched in an organisation, leading to intense bitterness and acrimony. Avoid such situations and such organisations at any cost. You have nothing to gain and much to lose if you get involved in this kind of unproductive and very disruptive activity.

2

Rumours, gossip, and innuendo

These are activities which should have no part in anyone's working day. Unfortunately, they are part and parcel of the working day in many organisations.

My advice is to ignore any rumours and gossip that are relayed to you. Avoid passing on any of this information, as you can easily become seen as part of the problem, even if you didn't initiate the rumour in the first place.

People who spread rumours and who gossip are troublemakers and have an insidious effect on any organisation they are part of. Such people are invariably part of the problem and never part of the solution. In my experience, the best solution for an organisation with serial offenders in this area is to take strong, decisive disciplinary action to root this problem out as soon as possible. Otherwise, this problem will continue to fester and may even become widespread throughout the organisation. Either way, you need to avoid such people as you have nothing to gain and much to lose if you associate with them.

Innuendo is not as obvious as rumours and gossip, but it can be equally damaging for the individual at the receiving end. If you are on the receiving end of innuendo, it is very hurtful and could become damaging to you if it is allowed to continue unabated. Call it out early if you can, or report it to your boss or HR before this troublemaking behaviour becomes established and your life at work and potentially your personal life become badly affected as a result.

3

Moaning, bitching, and complaining

All companies and organisations are vulnerable to this type of activity and some badly-run organisations are rife with it. Management needs to be vigilant in their recruitment practices to ensure that they do not recruit people with these tendencies into a company. If such people do manage to get through the recruitment process, management should be able to identify them during their probationary period and manage them out of the organisation at that stage.

If you encounter a person or some people like this in your company, give them a very wide berth as these people are to be avoided at any cost.

Similarly, take steps to avoid people who complain about everything but never put forward constructive solutions. Such people are a drain on companies and their fellow employees. They can drag an organisation down.

Naturally, some good people can resort to complaining in badly-run businesses. If you find yourself in such a company, you should move on because it could be years before the issues are addressed. Meanwhile, you would be better off working in a well-managed business rather than being dragged down in a poorly run business characterised by low morale and high levels of employee dissatisfaction.

4

Bullying

Bullying at work is something that all reputable employers are committed to preventing and eliminating.

It is insidious behaviour that must be comprehensively rooted out once it comes to light. However, this statement highlights one of the main difficulties with bullying, i.e. it is often hidden in an organisation and may only come to light weeks, months or even years after the bullying has occurred.

As a new employee, you need to be vigilant that you do not allow yourself to be bullied in either an overt or a covert manner. If someone attempts to bully you and you feel strong enough, you could call the bully out and advise them that you will report them if they continue to attempt to bully you. If you do not feel strong enough to confront the bully, report them to your boss or HR. Do not internalise the incident because if you fail to act promptly and decisively, it will recur because that is the way bullies operate.

If you see someone else being bullied and you feel strong enough, you could call the bully out. Alternatively, you could inform the person being bullied of their rights and advise them to speak to their boss or HR. Either way, the bully must not be allowed to continue this destructive and despicable behaviour.

In my experience, ALL bullies are cowards, and they usually back down when confronted. If they do not, you must report them.

The situation becomes much more complicated if the bully happens to be your boss. In that situation if you feel strong enough, you could advise them if they persist, you will take the matter to their boss or HR. If the situation persists after you have spoken to your boss's manager or HR, then there may well be a bullying culture in the organisation. This may suggest you should look for a new position in another, more reputable organisation where bullying of any type is not tolerated. I do accept and understand that most new employees who are bullied by a boss may feel they have no option but to look for another job rather than report the matter. While this is very understandable, it is regrettable, especially as the problem is likely to recur when you leave and your replacement is recruited.

5
Jokes, slagging/sledging, and banter

On the face of it, these may not seem to you to be obvious issues you need to concern yourself with. Unfortunately, if that is your opinion, you are mistaken as some jokes can easily constitute bullying, even if bullying was not intended by the person telling the joke.

Similarly, someone may consider slagging as part of the cut and thrust of a day's work. However, you need to be aware that what may be considered funny at the start of your career may be considered unacceptable a few years later because of changes in employment law or major changes in societal attitudes. In my own career, I saw a sea change in what was considered acceptable at the start of my career compared to the situation forty years later.

In today's world of increasing diversity at work, jokes and slagging can easily and are much more likely to offend than they would have done in the past. In addition, because the rights of different groups are now firmly enshrined in employment law, people are much less likely to put up with jokes and comments that have a discriminatory dimension to them. In any event, my strong advice to you is not to pass on a joke that could offend a fellow employee.

I do not wish to come across as a complete killjoy in addressing the subject of banter, as I enjoyed a bit of banter at work as much as anyone. Good-natured banter can greatly lighten the mood at work, but like the other points in this topic, it can easily morph into something that can offend when no offence is intended. Again, it is something to be aware of.

6

Cliques

I would advise against falling into a clique at work, especially if that group is comprised mainly of people in your own department. Understandably, you may often go on coffee breaks or lunch breaks with people in your own department but try to avoid going with the same people all of the time.

The danger is if you are with the same people all of the time, your group will become seen as a clique that people from other departments may feel unwelcome to approach.

In my opinion, you should try to get to know as many people as possible within the company. You should be free and also feel welcome to join any group at break time. It also makes work a more interesting and varied experience when you are not with the same small group all of the time.

Being able to mix with others can also help you in your working day, if as is increasingly the case, you will have to interact with people from other departments.

7
Socialising with colleagues

It is nice to socialise with your work colleagues after work on occasion. It often happens that some of your work colleagues become your friends, and these friendships may endure long after you or they have moved on from your initial employer. However, if you socialise with your work colleagues, try to avoid talking shop outside work as you never really get away from work in that type of situation.

Some multinational companies actively encourage socialising with colleagues, and some even carry it to extremes where employees feel it is expected that they should socialise with their work colleagues. I recommend that you avoid getting sucked into that kind of culture as it will only result in your social life being an extension of your working life.

As mentioned earlier, I would caution against losing touch with the people you used to socialise with before you started your first job or some people from your own village, town, or city. Again, it is good to have diversity in your circle of friends, as it helps to make you a more rounded individual.

8

Office parties

Office parties can be very enjoyable events and a great way to let off steam after a demanding year or after successfully completing some major project. However, I must caution you to bear one thing in mind when you are attending office parties, particularly, Christmas parties. My advice to you is that even though you are at a social event, you are still effectively at work as it involves work colleagues.

I realise this is a real killjoy piece of advice, but it is based on years of attending parties in large and small companies, often where there was a lot of free drink involved. Invariably, inhibitions are set aside as the night goes on. People may find themselves in situations which they haven't planned for and which they may subsequently regret. This can sometimes cause a person to feel that they may be better off leaving a job they had previously enjoyed working in because of the embarrassment caused by events they got involved in, which originated at a Christmas party.

This can be compounded nowadays by the invasiveness of social media, which can result in very embarrassing images being circulated to work colleagues or to a more general audience. Due to the negative publicity which has arisen from Christmas parties in recent years, most progressive employers have taken steps to curtail free bars at parties, and they often arrange taxis to ensure that people get home safely.

Be vigilant. Do not do anything at a company event that you may subsequently regret but not be allowed to forget.

9
Biases, prejudices, and blind spots

This is a challenging piece of advice to give anyone because, invariably, people are unaware of having these issues or if they are aware of them, they may not realise the extent to which they may influence their dealings with others. Because of this, they are unlikely to be aware of just how obvious these traits are to others until someone brings it to their attention.

If you have some unhelpful traits that you were previously unaware of and that have been brought to your attention, you need to address these issues because if they remain unchecked, they could have the potential to affect your relationships with colleagues. Equally so, if these issues remain unchecked, they may affect your judgment, and this, in turn, could affect your ability to make rational decisions in current and future roles.

Ideally, the very awareness of the issue will help you to address it, but if it is deeply embedded in your personality, you may need some professional counselling to help you to address and resolve this issue fully.

The cumulative effect of these unresolved issues could be to put progress in your job and career on hold if they are not addressed.

10
Non-work-related discussions at work

Subjects such as religion and politics are potentially divisive and should be avoided. They should certainly be dropped if they become unpleasant, as can easily happen with so much diversity in the workplace nowadays.

It is challenging enough to retain good working relationships in a demanding work environment without unnecessarily making this more difficult by introducing controversial topics or joining a discussion on controversial topics introduced by others.

My advice is to steer the conversation away from the potentially divisive issue or slip away quietly before you become embroiled in something that can readily get out of hand. Remember, such matters have nothing to do with the goals and objectives you have been recruited to achieve.

11
Talk v email to resolve disagreements

In a typical week, you will have at least one disagreement with other employees. Most of these will be healthy disagreements regarding the best way to handle some issue, and the vast majority of them will be readily resolved.

However, sometimes people can take entrenched positions on an issue, or sometimes things may get personal between you and a colleague you just do not get on with. In these kinds of situations, I would strongly encourage you to make every effort to resolve the issue through discussion with the person concerned. At least try this course of action before or even rather than involving third parties or reverting to email to outline your position in unequivocal terms.

If you can resolve the matter through discussion, this may result in you both developing some mutual respect which can help in your future dealings with that person. However, once the matter becomes committed to print, positions can become more deeply entrenched. Even if the matter is subsequently resolved in your favour, the relationship with this individual may be irretrievably damaged. This may be more serious if your role will require future dealings with that person. Remember when I spoke about always looking for win/win outcomes, such disagreements are a case in point.

In general, speaking to someone usually gives rise to less disagreement and less potential for misinterpretation than emailing the person. For this reason, I strongly recommend it. In the last few years, I have noticed a tendency for some people to write to people with whom they actually share an office. This strikes me as bizarre but does seem to be indicative of the tendency for some younger employees to email rather than talk to someone. Please do not go down that route unless it becomes the only course of action open to you.

12

Supporting your boss

In general, I recommend new employees should support their boss unless the boss is advocating a course of action that is unprofessional or unethical.

A typical boss will 'have your back,' especially as they get to know you as you settle into the company. It is natural that there should be a quid pro quo and that you should support them in most situations unless you firmly believe they are wrong about something. In that case, I would suggest you raise the matter privately with them in the first instance and hopefully resolve the disagreement readily at that stage.

If you cannot reach an agreement and if the matter is fundamental to the running of the company or your department, you may decide you have no alternative but to pursue your career elsewhere. Unless your boss is completely out of order, such a drastic course of action should not be necessary.

13

Looking for a salary increase

Usually, you won't have to do this as your employment contract will specify when your first salary increase will be due.

However, you may feel you have to address this matter if you are performing very well and you have also taken on additional duties. Alternatively, you may decide to address the matter if you have been headhunted by another company that is willing to offer you a substantial salary increase.

If you decide to address this matter with your boss, you should be clear on the specific reasons that you believe you are worth the pay increase you are requesting. If you have taken on additional duties, they would need to be substantial to justify looking for a salary increase before the due date.

Remember, your boss may have given you these extra duties to accelerate your development and may not appreciate you using them as leverage to negotiate a salary increase so soon. In addition, if you are happy with the job and the company, you need to think about whether you are willing to leave all of that behind you to join another company that may not be as suitable for you as your present employer.

Generally, I would advise against changing jobs solely for financial reasons at any time, but particularly in the first year or two with your initial employer.

Before you ask for a salary increase, you will need to have fully thought through what action you will take if your request for a salary increase is turned down. Will you leave the company? Or, if you stay, will the psychological contract with your employer be damaged? These are things you need to be clear about if you are going to bring up this delicate matter before you are due a salary increase.

If another company offers you a salary which is clearly above the market rate, you need to understand that if you accept the job offer that your new employer will probably slow down or reduce your subsequent salary increases in order to ensure that your salary is not out of line with the rest of their workforce.

14
Dealing with a salary cut

Sometimes employees are confronted with a situation where their employer may ask them to take a pay reduction because of a downturn in the economy, a loss of market share, or the failure of a new product in the market. Any or all of these could cause your employer to cut your salary as part of a cost reduction programme.

You will need to consider your position closely in such a scenario. If a downturn in the economy is giving rise to the proposal, you may decide to stay with the company as the position may well be the same as most other competitors in your sector.

However, if the problem is caused by poor management, you may decide to accept the pay cut, but at the same time, you may also decide to begin looking for a new job with a more successful company in the same sector. Either way, think the matter through and be clear on the reasons for your chosen course of action. Do not be overly influenced by your colleagues, as all employees have their own values and beliefs. You need to act on your reasons rather than on theirs.

15
Dealing with a lay-off

My advice here would be similar to the previous point. If the lay-off is caused by some national or international event, such as the COVID-19 pandemic, this is outside the control of your employer. Providing the employer is handling this matter professionally and is treating you and your fellow employees with dignity, I would suggest you double down and try to manage your way through it. Any support you get from your employer to assist you with your physical and mental health reflects well on them, and their efforts to make you and your colleagues feel important and valued.

However, if the lay-off has been precipitated by mismanagement, you may decide to stay in the short term, but you may also decide to commence the search for a new position in a more professionally managed company.

16

Online scams and viruses

Young professionals are usually aware of these dangers, but online scams are becoming increasingly sophisticated, and many of them can look authentic, especially if they appear to come from your bank or the revenue commissioners. The bottom line is to delete them if they look for your credit card details. As a general rule, try to unsubscribe from all unwanted mail even though some sources do not provide that facility, or where they do, it doesn't always work.

It is easy to allow viruses to corrupt your online data inadvertently. Simply clicking on an attachment to an email can introduce a virus into your computer that can cause you to lose years of valuable work. This danger is more acute now because some computer hackers seem to have nothing better to do than to corrupt companies' computer records. The danger of being the victim of an online virus is greater now with people working from home since the COVID-19 pandemic. This is something that companies are being forced to address where virus protection systems are not as robust in employees' homes as they are in the office. The bottom line is not to open attachments you are unsure of and unsubscribe from anything you do not want.

17
Social media at work

Most companies have clear policies advising employees not to use social media during working hours, and some have clear guidelines in their company handbook to ensure that employees adhere to this policy.

I strongly advise you not to use social media at work unless it is directly relevant to your work, and you are specifically asked to use it in a one-off situation. You are paid to meet the objectives of your position and using social media at work for most professionals is strictly forbidden. Using social media in an unauthorised manner is effectively stealing from your employer as you are doing something that is not part of your employment contract while ignoring duties and responsibilities that are part of that contract.

Some employers turn a blind eye to a certain amount of this behaviour. I firmly believe these employers are ill-advised in tolerating this, especially as there have been numerous cases reported where bullying at work took place across social media platforms. In reality, such employees were committing two dismissible offences simultaneously, i.e. bullying at work and using social media at work.

Unless explicitly directed otherwise, you must always confine your use of social media to your personal time. Anything else is a serious abuse of your contract of employment and could lead to your immediate dismissal.

18
Time off from work

In general, try to look for as little time off from work during the day as possible.

If you need time off to visit a doctor, a dentist, or to attend something else that can only be done during office hours, please make up the time later in the day or later in the week.

You do not want to acquire a reputation of being an employee who takes more than they give, as that will limit your prospects in most companies.

19

Personal calls at work

The same applies to taking personal calls at work. Try to take calls only when it is absolutely necessary. Encourage friends and family not to call you at work unless it is essential. You can always call people back on your mobile at break time, which is usually satisfactory for whoever calls you.

With nearly everyone having a mobile phone nowadays, there is no excuse for wasting time at work on personal calls. Remember, if you do this, you are sending out the wrong message to your employer and your colleagues.

20
Developing a long-term view

One of the things that any new employee needs to learn is that they will experience many challenging days and many setbacks throughout their career. As well as having the resilience to deal with these, you need to learn when to let go of an issue until another day and when to let go of something altogether.

The employees who develop the judgment to develop this long-term view are the people who have long and successful careers. Often this may be with a very limited number of companies throughout their working life.

To use an analogy, this is often a case of being prepared to lose the battle to win the war. Employees who can see the bigger picture can take this long-term view. These people are survivors, and they provide much-needed continuity for any company, especially in one that may experience high staff turnover. Such people are also role models for young professionals who may be surprised by how many setbacks and how much critical feedback they have to absorb in the early years of their careers. They may be wondering whether they will ever be able to build a career in this company or this sector. These long-serving professionals can help young professionals see beyond their present difficulties and help them to take a long-term view. In my opinion, you have much to learn from these seasoned professionals.

Conclusion

Since I started writing this book, the entire world has been dramatically affected by the COVID-19 pandemic. The world of work has not escaped the influence of the pandemic. The changes which have arisen since the onset of COVID-19 have revolutionised the world of work, as much as, if not more than all of the technological advances of the past fifty years. Even though we have now entered the endemic phase of the pandemic it is unlikely we will ever return to the traditional model of the five day week in an office environment.

Even allowing for the changes brought about by COVID-19 the advice in this book is likely to remain relevant to you as you embark on your working life. People will still have to manage the transition from the world of college to the world of work, even if that world of work may involve working at home on a full or part-time basis for many employees. People will still have to decide what success at work means for them, and they will also have to keep that decision under periodic review as their personal circumstances change.

I am aware there is a lot of advice in this book and that if you read through it in one or two sittings, you may well be feeling a little overwhelmed by the challenges involved in adjusting to the world of work. It is important that you remember all of the challenges you have faced in your life to date and that you look at this as just one more challenge for you to overcome.

Finally, I would like to conclude by wishing you every success and happiness in your first job and in your working life. As I said in my introduction to the book, if this book helps you in any way, I will be delighted.

Good luck!

Colman Collins

Leabharlanna Poiblí Chathair Baile Átha Cliath
Dublin City Public Libraries

Please Review

Dear Reader,

If you enjoyed this book, would you kindly post a short review on Goodreads or on whichever online store you purchased the book from? Your feedback will make all the difference to getting the word out about this book.

Thank you in advance.

Colman